ECO WINNERS

ECO WINNERS

UNCOVERING THE TRAITS OF SUCCESSFUL ENVIRONMENTAL LEADERS

KATYA PRONICHENKO

NEW DEGREE PRESS
COPYRIGHT © 2020 KATYA PRONICHENKO
All rights reserved.

ECO WINNERS
Uncovering the Traits of Successful Environmental Leaders

ISBN 978-1-64137-520-7 *Paperback*
      978-1-64137-521-4 *Kindle Ebook*
      978-1-64137-522-1 *Ebook*

*Dedicated to my family and friends that
continue to support me in my mission*

CONTENTS

INTRODUCTION		9
BECOMING AN ECO-WINNER WITH THIS BOOK		15

PART 1.	**ECO-HISTORY**	**17**
CHAPTER 1.	A YOUNG AND RESTLESS CLIMATE	19
CHAPTER 2.	THE EARTH NOW	27
CHAPTER 3.	DEALING WITH WASTE	37
CHAPTER 4.	EXPLORING FOOD AND ENERGY	45
CHAPTER 5.	WHY WE SHOULD STAY POSITIVE	55

PART 2.	**ECO-WINNERS**	**63**
CHAPTER 6.	EXTREMISM—AN ECO-WINNER TRAIT	65
CHAPTER 7.	GRASSROOTS TO NOBEL PEACE PRIZE	73
CHAPTER 8.	THE IMPACT OF A STUDENT	83
CHAPTER 9.	FIXING THE BROKEN FOOD SYSTEM ONE FARM AT A TIME	95
CHAPTER 10.	WORKING FROM THE INSIDE	101
CHAPTER 11.	SUPPORTING ECO-WINNERS	111

PART 3.	**ECO-WORLD**	**119**
CHAPTER 12.	THE POWER OF VOLUNTEERS	121
CHAPTER 13.	THE POWER OF WORKING WITH, NOT AGAINST	129

CHAPTER 14. ECO-COMPANIES AND ECO-INDUSTRY	137
CHAPTER 15. CORPORATIONS ≠ EVIL	143
CHAPTER 16. ECO-COUNTRIES CREATED BY ECO-WINNERS	151
CONCLUSION. TIME TO STEP UP	161
BIBLIOGRAPHY	165

INTRODUCTION

"What do you wake up to do?"

It was my sophomore year of high school and my older brother was graduating from Babson College. The speaker, a curly-brown-haired woman, was delivering a speech about entrepreneurship. Standing in front of the entire graduating class of students, she asked everyone, "What is your purpose? What do you wake up to do?"

For weeks, those words rattled around in my mind, popping up at random times and locations.

I had been the average stressed out overachiever, taking all the hardest classes I could and stuffing every day with extracurriculars—swimming, DECA, piano, choir, Russian School, you get it. As soon as I finished one activity, I would already be running to the next one. Soon enough, the question was shoved to the back of my mind, forgotten as I busied myself with life and school. However, this question resurfaced on the last day of junior year, when I got a biopsy of my thyroid.

The biopsy was positive, and I was diagnosed with cancer.

In an instant, all the thoughts that used to have so much importance—grades, extracurriculars, and college—flew out the window. At that moment, I remember sitting in the doctor's office and thinking only one thought:

I have so much left to do in the world.

At the time, I did not know how much time I had left to live. Being put in a life-or-death situation forced me to see very clearly what I truly wanted to do. It revealed to me the true purpose of my life, or the **thing I wake up to do.** My old cycle of living life through stress and competition was overhauled as I could only process the present moment. And in the present moment, I understood that I did not care about the things I put such emphasis on in the past.

I understood that my purpose in life was to make the world a greener, more harmonious, and just place. This realization led me to rethink my everyday life choices and to live a life more consistent with my ideals.

Now, I try to live my life in accordance to my favorite Rumi quote: "Yesterday I was clever, so I wanted to change the world. Today I am wise, so I am changing myself."

I have since started to volunteer with the Sierra Club by clearing trails and planting trees after California wildfires. I reached out and then interned with my local government to try to inspire green legislation. I worked with my community's Resource Conservation district to plant oak trees and milkweed for monarch butterflies.

As I watered the last oak tree seedling, I felt that I was, albeit in a small way, making the Earth greener, one seedling at a time. When I wanted government action, my friend and I went to the office of Los Angeles Councilmember Mike Bonin. Through talking to the councilmember and his staff, we were able to inspire legislation that increased urban forestry in Los Angeles. Whenever I shared the benefits of sustainability with my friends and family, and especially when I led by example, I felt fulfilled. My small actions created a green chain reaction. These experiences, when put together, made me feel hopeful.

On this journey of volunteering and outreach, I realized that there were other individuals who were on the same mission. They volunteered and lived eco-friendly lives—impacting real change in their communities. These individuals amazed me with their seemingly infinite passion and commitment to their goals. I came to see these individuals as eco-winners, environmental leaders who have left a positive impact on the Earth and are committed to protecting the planet in whatever way they can.

That's when the idea of sharing the stories of these eco-winners hit me.

In *Eco Winners,* I will explore the stories of environmental leaders and how they use different strategies to make their projects so successful. I have spent the last year researching, discussing, and examining the impacts of numerous environmental trailblazers, including volunteers, interest group workers, green government officials, and global leaders who have had and continue to have a profound impact on the world.

This book is written in three parts.

Part 1: **Eco-History** contains the incredible story of Greta Thunberg and chapters that give an overview of how Earth's resources have been overused throughout history. Throughout this section, you will learn about major events that transformed the Earth and how we now use and abuse it, including insights into the First Agricultural Revolution, the Industrial Revolution, and the current agricultural and energy markets.

Part 2: **Eco-Winners** covers Chapters 6 to 11 in which I explore the stories of activists in environmental movements, ranging from beach cleanups and tree-plantings to protesting destructive pipelines and petitioning the government. One of my favorite moments was when I interviewed a recent college graduate not much older than me who, to my surprise, had already been arrested twice for her environmental activism and manually tried to stop the building of a pipeline. Some other eco-stories include:

- Wangari Maathai: a Kenyan woman who founded the Green Belt movement, inspiring rural African women to plant millions of trees and oppose the unsustainable dictatorship regime.
- Heidi Harmon: the mayor of San Luis Obispo, who went from being a discouraged single mother to the leader of multiple environmental marches and organizations,

eventually becoming one of the main green legislators in Central California.

Part 3: **Eco-World** contains Chapters 12 to 16. In these chapters, I explore the impact of different environmental organizations including the Environmental Defense Fund, Sierra Club, and companies including Amazon, Unilever, and more. These chapters highlight the importance of companies and governments, and how an individual person can influence both to be more sustainable.

From researching and conducting interviews, I have derived that all eco-winners share four C-traits of environmental advocacy success.

Four "C" Traits
1. Commitment
2. Confidence
3. Consistency
4. Creativity

These traits, although simple, are what characterize the success of eco-winners. I have seen that not only do these individuals have the drive to sustain their advocacy—be it clean air, water, or community involvement—but they also possess creativity and unwavering persistence, which pushes them to never give up on their goals. Whether these leaders started their missions with almost no resources, money, education, or experience; their commitment, confidence, consistency, and creativity are what allows them to make their impact.

By writing about these eco-winners, I understood that there is no reason that I cannot make my own impact. In fact, I realized that I have underestimated the true **power of the individual.** I saw that my biggest resources for accomplishing my goals were the like-minded eco-winners that I could learn from and work with.

Real societal change *is* possible, and we are here to prove it. As you learn with me through this book about the extraordinary people that fill this Earth, I hope to show that everyone, including young people like me, *can* leave an impact on this beautiful planet.

I will leave you with one of my favorite quotes by the environmentalist Jane Goodall.

"You cannot get through a single day without having an impact on the world around you. What you do makes a difference and you have to decide what kind of a difference you want to make."
—JANE GOODALL

BECOMING AN ECO-WINNER WITH THIS BOOK

This book is made to inspire the young and the old, the new and the knowledgeable, to take more action in environmental advocacy. Hence, this book is what you make of it. Below are some suggestions to help you make the most of this book.

IDENTIFY WHAT YOU CARE ABOUT
This entire book is about being inspired by the stories of eco-winners and finding your own mission and impact in environmental advocacy. To do that, people must be positive that they can make a difference. Before you begin reading this book, **write down five different aspects of the Earth you want to change.** Then, as you read, look for the answers on how other eco-winners have addressed those same problems.

UNDERSTAND YOUR POWER

Are you a student, an educator, a parent? How can you contribute to making this planet a greener place? **Write down two ways you can be more sustainable.** Do these seem insignificant or impossible? Keep these strategies in mind as you read the case studies and statistics throughout this book. By the time you are finished reading, I hope you will see how much power an individual really has.

TAKE ACTION!

The point of this book is to inspire you to incorporate advocacy into your life, whether this means eating more sustainably, shopping less, volunteering at clean-ups or with interest groups, getting involved in the government, donating to green organizations, etc. I hope that this book will help you understand that you are not alone in your efforts. Every effort matters, whether you start with changing your own consumption habits or inspire others to do so. The secret to success then, is starting small, enrolling others, and steadily working toward a collective goal, exactly as all the eco-winners have done. Every big movement starts with a small grassroots project, and action is what will get us closer to a greener Earth.

1

ECO-HISTORY

CHAPTER 1

A YOUNG AND RESTLESS CLIMATE

You are never too small to make a difference.

—GRETA THUNBERG

In March 2019, Greta Thunberg, a sixteen-year-old Swedish student, was nominated for the Nobel Peace Prize for founding the Youth Strike for Climate movement.[1] Thunberg first found out about climate change from her parents when she was just eight years old. Even at such a young age, she recalls feeling disillusioned with the state of the Earth and government inaction. At the age of eleven, Thunberg fell into depression and became mute. Later, she was diagnosed with Asperger syndrome and selective mutism, a condition that allowed her to speak only when absolutely necessary. Thunberg says that she "feels like she is dying if she does not protest."[2]

Her undying commitment compelled her to take action. Thunberg began her global environmental movement by skipping school to protest. In August 2018, at the age of fifteen, Thunberg spent her days outside of the Swedish Parliament holding a sign that read "*Skolstrejk för Klimatet,*" meaning "School Strike for the Climate." Day after day, Thunberg would come back to strike, gaining the support of other activists. Soon enough, the media started to take notice and her movement grew in size and popularity as other students joined her in protest.

After a month of consistent protesting, Thunberg's strikes developed into a national movement for students to advocate for climate reform. In November 2018, she organized the national Swedish climate strike in which thousands of students marched, demanding environmental legislation from local and federal governments. As news spread, students all over the world were inspired to strike, snowballing into an international movement with strikes in over seventy-two countries.[3] These strikes continued to grow, and in March of the following year, Greta led the next global climate strike with 1.4 million students from 112 countries joining the movement.[4]

In the sixteen months since Thunberg first started her advocacy, she has addressed heads of state at the United Nations,[5] met with the Pope, sparred with President Donald Trump, and inspired the largest global climate strike demonstration in human history. She has been celebrated in murals and books and compared to Joan of Arc.[6]

Thunberg striking in front of the Swedish parliament[7]

UNCOVERING THUNBERG'S MOVEMENT: MINDSET
When I first read Thunberg's story, I was blown away. Was one girl powerful enough to create a global movement? How did she do it? I decided to uncover the traits of advocates like Thunberg so I could learn how to effectively change the world.

One of the first things that propelled Thunberg's advocacy was her unique way of understanding the Earth's existing conditions. Partly because of the uncommon perspective afforded to her by her medical conditions, she felt the threat of climate change more strongly than the average person. To her, climate change and government inaction is a tragedy that needs to be addressed. For her, there was nothing more important than mitigating further climate change.

This type of "black and white activism," in which one sees their goals in extremes, usually takes different forms in activists. After my cancer diagnosis, I saw my own ideals become more extreme. I recognized that I had adopted a clearer, more dedicated stance toward protecting the Earth. My diagnosis made me see what limited time we have left and reminded me to stop putting off my goals and act.

Thunberg also kept a mindset of hope. Instead of getting discouraged by the realities of climate change, she remained optimistic in her efforts to protect the planet. This hope is what kept her activism alive. Even in the midst of disillusionment, eco-winners remain hopeful and **confident** in their efforts, finding the balance between understanding Earth's problems and being inspired to be part of the solution. At present, many people are experiencing cognitive dissonance, feeling like the world does not fit together anymore. This ideology only disheartens and prevents youth from realizing their own potential to make change.

I see this mindset in many people, including myself. Before I starting volunteering, I thought that with increasing time and energy spent on advocacy, people would have less faith in their ability to disrupt the system and make a difference.

However, the more I volunteered, the more I met people who inspired me with their work and efforts. With these new relationships, I felt more hopeful for the future because I knew that people like me were fighting for the same goal. These people became my resources, people I looked up to and supported. As one of my friends from the Sierra Club mentioned, "It is both about what you are doing and about what you can do. Humans took over the world, something that seemed almost impossible; advances that were unthinkable tens of years ago are now possible." The world is full of possibility. We have the resources and solutions; we just have to use them to go make our impact.

Greta Thunberg is an eco-winner. She consistently advocates for change, and even when she was starting out and striking alone, she had no fear in mind that her efforts were useless or would go unheard. Instead, she led by example. Her firm beliefs and consistent activism inspires others and continues to lead activists to become a considerable force to be reckoned with. The four main traits that make Thunberg a powerful eco-winner are her commitment, consistency, confidence, and creativity.

1. **Commitment**

Without her commitment, Thunberg's extreme views would have never manifested as action. She saw the environmental climate crisis as an emergency that needs to be fixed right away, but without her commitment to fix this goal, Thunberg would not have gotten the results of a global climate strike movement. What made Thunberg so successful is that she acted on the issue without hesitation and saw her goals through to the end, no matter the setbacks.

2. **Consistency**

We must not wait for others, whether it is governments or companies, to act for the environment; instead, we should act at our own level and inspire others. Thunberg embodies this concept. She consistently showed up to strike day after day, even when she stood alone. Even now, Thunberg continues to strike every Friday, inspiring thousands of students worldwide to do the same. Being consistent means upholding your beliefs—doing what you can to be environmentally friendly in other aspects of your life and constantly educating yourself. Thunberg's sustainable vision is evident in every aspect of her life. In addition to her climate movement, she is vegan and has inspired her friends and family to do the same. Thunberg showcases how being consistent in all areas of your life amplifies your impact to make a big difference.

3. Confidence

If Thunberg had no confidence, the climate strike movement would have died long ago. Instead of giving up, she believed in the power of the individual. At fifteen years of age, she was sure of her goal and did not back down, believing that if adults were not doing enough, she would. We see this trait of confidence in practically every successful leader, whether it is Mahatma Gandhi, Martin Luther King Jr., Cesar Chavez, or Dolores Huerta, Thunberg makes me question my own belief in the individual: Would I have had the confidence to strike alone? Would I still believe in my movement if it did not bring immediate change?

4. Creativity in Problem Solving

Thunberg created a movement that was influenced solely by students and people her own age, magnifying the voices of young people. Not only does this show that activists can possess a considerable political power, but it shows how important it is to creatively use the resources at your disposal to exert the maximum influence.

The student climate strike movement became so powerful because Thunberg did not back down, and when other like-minded students were inspired to join, they created an even greater momentum. My mom always tells me "People can see everything," and I think this is true. When Thunberg silently stood for her beliefs, a like-minded community acknowledged and made something of it. Without those that supported Thunberg's vision, this global movement would have never been realized. In one of her speeches, Thunberg explains that solving the environmental crisis is going to be one of the hardest issues we have ever faced, but with the combined effort of activists, we can take on anything.[8]

In 2019, Thunberg sailed from Sweden to New York to speak at the UN Climate Action Summit, which hosted representatives from 192 nation-states and aimed to promote further global environmental governance. There, Thunberg conveyed the message, "We will be watching you." She was speaking for the new generation of students and the future generation of eco-winners.

She addressed the reality that climate change, pollution, the collapse of ecosystems, and mass extinction will soon be irreversible if countries and individuals do not act on these problems now. Thunberg called government representatives to action, reminding leaders that the younger generation will hold them accountable for any climate pledges they make.[9] As a result of the Climate Action Summit, seventy-seven countries committed to cutting greenhouse gases to net zero by 2050, and seventy countries announced that they will boost their national action plans by 2020.[10]

TAKEAWAYS

The fact that Thunberg, a teenager, has already influenced global environmental governance is incredibly inspiring. From her advocacy on the streets of Stockholm, to her leadership in international climate strikes and her spokesmanship at summits, Thunberg's influence can be felt worldwide. She is a constant reminder that we can maximize our individual power to all become eco-winners in our own right.

Small acts, when multiplied by millions of people, can transform the world.
—HOWARD ZINN

CHAPTER 2

THE EARTH NOW

"Now that we have learned to fly in the air like birds and dive in the sea like fish, only one thing remains—to learn to live on Earth like humans."

—GEORGE BERNARD SHAW

The Earth has been modified and influenced by humans starting from the beginning of history. As the human population has increased throughout time, so has the pressure on the environment and its resources. In this chapter, I introduce how we got to where we are now, and why we need drastic environmental change.

1. First Agricultural Revolution

The disruption of Earth's natural resources started with the first Agricultural Revolution. From 10,000 to 2,000 BC in the Middle East and Asia, many hunter-gatherer societies transitioned to sedentary farming lifestyles. With this development, individuals no longer traveled for their source of food and, consequently, lands and resources became exploited for growing civilizations. Societies such as the Byzantine Empire overused the area's resources and caused desertification, the changing of green, productive land into desert. The invention of bronze axes hastened widespread deforestation and many ancient shoreline cities including Troy, Mycenae, and Ephesus are now miles inland as soil erosion from deforestation extended the coastal plains. Similarly, as early as the first century AD, problems like overfishing were recorded near Rome.[1]

2. Industrial Revolution

Since the time humans have inhabited the Earth, the Industrial Revolution has caused the most significant change on the global climate and environment.

The Industrial Revolution began in the late 1700s with the creation and expansion of coal-powered machines in England and Western Europe. During that time, water, wood, and then coal became commonly used to power machines, and the rapid growth of machinery prompted the increased mining and extraction of these resources. Factories burning coal released carbon dioxide and particulates into the atmosphere, contributing to pollution in cities. As the population grew, so did the demand for machine-made products and natural resources.

THE ANTHROPOCENE

Since then, technology has rapidly expanded and the human population has skyrocketed. Just in the past 300 years, the human population has increased to over seven billion and is expected to reach ten billion in this century. Currently, humans exploit 30 to 50 percent of the Earth's land. Tropical rainforests are disappearing at a fast pace, and with them their biodiversity. More than half of all accessible fresh water is used by humans. Dam building and river diversion restricts the natural migration of fish and breaks aquatic ecosystems. More than two-thirds of the world's fish are overfished and depleted, and fisheries have removed more than 25 percent of the primary food source for marine life.[2] Energy usage has grown 16-fold during the twentieth century, causing the largest emissions up to date. Over 160 million tons of atmospheric sulfur dioxide per year, more than twice the sum of its natural emissions. Runoff nitrogen from fertilizers has spilled into rivers and bodies of water in higher amounts than is fixed naturally in all terrestrial ecosystems.[3] Carbon dioxide and methane are at their highest levels in the past 400 millennia due to fossil fuel burning and agriculture. The consequences of these emissions include acid precipitation, photochemical smog, and contamination of air and water.

The vast majority of these effects have been caused by "civilized nations," which constitute only about 25 percent of the entire human population. Despite this small percentage, the environmental repercussions have been far-reaching. According to the latest estimates by the Intergovernmental Panel on Climate Change (IPCC), the Earth's average temperature will increase by 3–8°F during this century.[4] For measure, the Earth was only 8–9°F cooler during the last Ice

Age.[5] This increase in temperature is mostly caused by the increase in greenhouse gases such as CO_2 and methane that trap heat inside our atmosphere.

We are now in the "Anthropocene" era, characterized by scientists as a human-dominated, geological epoch and the warmest period in the past ten to twelve millennia[6] caused by human-induced climate change. Many scientists now say we are headed toward the sixth extinction due to the increased rates of biodiversity loss.[7]

It is important to act on these matters now, and not wait for them to worsen. Carbon dioxide levels, the leading cause of climate change, will not stabilize until emissions are at a level where carbon sinks can absorb them. According to the National Research Council, that level requires an 80 percent drop in CO_2 emissions.[8] As long as humans put more CO_2 into the atmosphere, temperatures will continue to rise, and climate change will intensify. Many US policymakers argue that they "should wait and see whether climate change will cause any harm before undertaking policies to reduce emissions."[9] The flaw in this thinking is that it assumes and makes people believe that climate change can be quickly fixed when it becomes "serious enough." However, this vastly underestimates the current force of climate change and the delay of the climate's response to human-caused emissions.

In this turbulent time, humans can be the agents of change, starting with us. We can live within the boundaries of the Earth and be sustainable individuals, working together toward the goal of decreasing our impact on the environment.

Throughout history, the environmental movement has coevolved to address these problems.

THE BIRTH AND GROWTH OF THE US ENVIRONMENTALIST MOVEMENT

The first environmentalist sentiment in the United States arose during the Transcendentalism period in the mid-nineteenth century. For the first time, artists and writers demonstrated appreciation for nature and inspired others to see the environment as sacred and worth preserving. Transcendentalist, Henry David Thoreau, wrote, "In wildness is the preservation of the world."

The end of the nineteenth century marked the beginning of the United States' first conservation movement. In 1892, John Muir founded the Sierra Club, the first broad-based environmental organization. Then, in 1898, Gifford Pinchot became chief of the Division of Forestry, which later became the US Forestry Service; this program advocated for the sustainable management of forests and was one of the first environmental government initiatives. In 1905, the National Audubon Society was created, and the National Parks and Conservation Association followed in 1919.[10] The second wave of conservation happened during the New Deal—a series of relief programs and initiatives enacted by President Franklin D. Roosevelt after the Great Depression.[11] New environmental legislation during that time included the Taylor Grazing Act of 1934, which addressed overgrazing, and the creation of the Bureau of Land Management in 1946.

The third wave of conservation and environmental legislation followed in the 1950s and 60s. This wave focused more on the preservation of areas of natural beauty and less on the utilitarian aspects of rationing resources. Some of the legislation that was passed included the Wilderness Act of 1964, which preserved national forest land, the Land and Water Conservation Fund Act, which facilitated parks, and Congress's first federal water and air pollution control laws. In 1970, Nixon's presidency passed the National Environmental Policy Act (NEPA), which set off a period of environmental litigation. NEPA required federal agencies to submit Environmental Impact Statements for their projects, driving government initiatives to become more transparent. Furthermore, the 1972 Clean Water Act became the largest source of discretionary spending at the time, with money channeled to municipalities for facilities such as sewers and treatment plants. Other legislation included the 1973 Endangered Species Act, 1974 Safe Drinking Water Act, 1976 Resource Conservation and Recovery Act—all of which protected more land and decreased the high levels of pollution, biodiversity loss, and toxic waste.

Much of this environmental legislation was inspired by teach-ins and protests organized by environmentalists as well as by green politicians in the Senate and Congress.[13] The ninety-second Congress was known to be the most active in environmental and public health regulation. It focused on health, safety, and environmental quality issues and was enforced by the Environmental Protection Agency, the first national environmental governance force. The Environmental Protection Agency (EPA) opened up a more activist, reformist orientation within agencies and garnered participation from the public, who could now hold the government accountable.

However, in the 1980s, the Reagan Administration reversed most policy advances and since then, there have been no major US environmental laws passed.

Knowing that the US has had the potential to pass successful environmental legislation makes us question: Why is there no wave of environmental regulation right now, when it is most dire?

The answer to this question is complicated, specifically because many politicians are heavily involved in the same industries that hurt the environment and because corporations heavily influence policy. In the United States, businesses and corporate groups hire lobbyists and create interest groups to advance pro-business legislation that, in many cases, is harmful for the environment. For example, the effect of corporate lobbying can be seen in the 2009-10 Waxman Bill and the American Clean Energy Act, an energy bill that introduced both renewable energies and efficient energy methods to be implemented nationally. In total, companies spent more than $700 million lobbying the bill, and in the end, these companies' lobbying efforts killed the bill, which could have mitigated $60 billion in climate damages.[14]

Another major obstacle includes domestic intransigence, in which states are stubborn and refuse to change their beliefs to compromise on solutions. In the US, polarized parties often cannot compromise on universal environmental legislation.

Lastly, many government officials often come from and return to work in the private sector, where their own interests influence the legislation they support. Monsanto, the American agrochemical corporate giant, practically "controls both the White House and the US Congress."[12] Monsanto dominates a significant share of the agribusiness and genetically modified organism industries, both of which are heavily affected by the United States Department of Agriculture (USDA) and Food and Drug Administration (FDA) federal legislation. Because of this, Monsanto spends billions of dollars on efforts to keep the number of regulations low to maximize their profits. Numerous ex-Monsanto employees, particularly from lobbying and legal infrastructures, currently fill judicial, regulatory, and advisory positions within the US government, pushing through corrupt and concentrated interest legislation.[15] For example, Clarence Thomas used to work as an attorney for Monsanto. Now, as Supreme Court Justice, Thomas has ruled in favor of agribusiness and against their regulation. Furthermore, FDA Deputy Commissioner Michael Taylor worked as the vice president of Monsanto for four years. These public servants work in congruence with their interests, and this results in policy that is unfairly slanted in favor of industry and against the environment.

So, what can *we* do?

We as individuals can educate ourselves, vote for environmentally conscious candidates, and protest unsustainable and degrading politics. This way, we can fight for a greener Earth.

TAKEAWAYS

Current problems with the environment are immense, but fixable—for now. In the past, we have seen politicians respond to powerful environmental movements; however, no major environmental policies have been passed since the height of the last environmental wave. It is time to change that. Eco-winners can take advantage of this time in history and start fixing the Anthropocene's problems. We can do that in a variety of ways, taking cue from the eco-winners of past and current generations. We can vote, march, adopt more sustainable lifestyles, support environmental advocacy groups, and continue to take advantage of opportunities to advocate for the Earth in whatever ways we can.

CHAPTER 3

DEALING WITH WASTE

"We have forgotten how to be good guests, how to walk lightly on the earth as other creatures do."

—BARBARA WARD

Our inefficient and unsustainable ways of living have created a lot of waste that is now circling around the globe. In theory, there should be no waste. In nature, all matter serves as resources for organisms in the food chain, with animal and plant matter acting as nutrients for detritivores and their byproducts, soil. However, this is not the case.

The current problem is that we have a system in which obtaining resources is inefficient and creates waste that naturally should not be created. According to the 1989 study by Harris and Kneese, only 6 percent of the 10 tons of raw materials—including coal and wood—that are extracted for each person in the US every year end up in the durable products we use.[1] Additionally, according to the Lawrence Livermore National Laboratory, about 55 percent of all energy in the United States is wasted, much of it through heat waste such as the warm exhaust of automobiles or the energy produced by furnaces.[2] However, this does not have to be the case. Countries are maximizing their energy potential through implementing efficient energy systems. In 2018, the United States was ranked eighth among twenty-three of the world's top energy-consuming countries in efficiency, behind several European nations, China, and Japan.[3] Like energy, other resources including food and water are inefficiently used, which goes to show the need for new legislation to create more logical and sustainable systems to efficiently minimize waste.

1. **Food Waste**

Almost half of the food ready for harvest in the United States does not go toward feeding the population. Fourteen percent of the food that Americans actually buy is thrown out.[4] Globally, 30 percent of food is wasted across the supply chain, contributing 8 percent of total global greenhouse gas emissions. This means that if food waste were a country, it would come in third after the United States and China in terms of impact on global warming.[5] The animal agriculture industry contributes waste and pollution from fertilizers, antibiotics, and excretions. According to the Environmental Protection Agency, a single dairy cow produces 21.9 tons of defecation each year.[6]

2. **Ocean Waste**

Nearly 90 percent of the world's marine fish stocks are now exploited.[7] One-third of that fish supply goes toward feeding livestock in the animal agriculture industry, fueling the inefficiency in the system.[8] Because of this abusive system, ocean fish numbers today have been cut in half since 1970.[9] Furthermore, monofilament lines from fishing end up in oceans, taking over 450 years to decompose.

3. Water Waste

The meat industry has created most of the water waste that we have today. To produce just one pound of beef in the US, it takes more than 2,400 gallons of water to produce. In comparison, it takes only 25 gallons of water to grow 1 pound of wheat.[10] To put into perspective, you can save more water by not eating a pound of meat than you can by not showering for six months. This jarring disparity of water usage in meat production is one of the reasons changing your diet can be so powerful.

The other big problem with waste is that a lot of it exists… **and** it does not go away quickly. Americans produce roughly 7 pounds of trash per day per person, totaling 2,500 pounds of trash each year. Of that trash, 69 percent will end up in landfills.[11] So, not only is the average American throwing away too much stuff, but also most of that stuff will not decompose in a decade of their lifetime.[12]

Material Type	Decomposition Time
Compostable packaging	2–12 weeks
Paper towel / Newspaper	2–6 weeks
Food waste (orange peel, etc.)	5 months

Wool	1–5 years
Cartons (milk, etc.)	5 years
Plastic bag	10–20 years
Nylon fabric (usually in sporty clothes)	30–40 years
Leather	50 years
Tin can (in soda bottles)	50 years
Foamed plastic cup	50 years
Rubber boot sole	50–80 years
Foamed plastic buoy	80 years
Batteries	100 years
Plastic bottles	450 years
Monofilament fishing line (most common type of fishing line)	500 years
Glass bottle	1 million years

Most of the "stuff" we consume and then subsequently throw away ends up decomposing for decades. And because most products (and, therefore, trash) are made of materials that do not decompose quickly, landfills of waste exude methane, a greenhouse gas that is roughly thirty times more potent as a heat-trapping gas than carbon dioxide.[13]

However, waste and its toxic fumes can be decreased by changing our individual actions.

We can start by using easy-to-adopt alternatives for trash. For example, instead of using plastic utensils that have a decomposition time of ten to twenty years, you can use a set of reusable utensils. As for me, carrying my set of utensils brings me joy whenever I get to pull out my teal fork and spoon!

By being mindful of your own consumption and trying to avoid buying unsustainable goods, one can decrease their own carbon footprint. Being mindful can start whenever you ask yourself, "Do I really need a double-double in In-N-Out?" or "Do I really need a new iPhone?" which becomes easier over time. This way, you will live in a more environmentally friendly way and save some money as well, a win-win.

If you want a green future, **embody a green future.**

To do that, I would recommend following some of these tips to decrease your waste intake.

1. Reuse and repair
2. Make your own (DIY!)
3. Shop less
4. Phase out disposables
5. Switch to green products including green cleaners and other green alternatives
6. Use your own bags
7. Compost
8. Tackle energy and water waste through mindful eating

ECO-WINNER DECISION GUIDE
Here is a guide to help you make more sustainable choices in everyday life. Bookmark this page, take a picture, or just make a mental note to follow a frame of mindfulness when making decisions that will affect your carbon footprint.

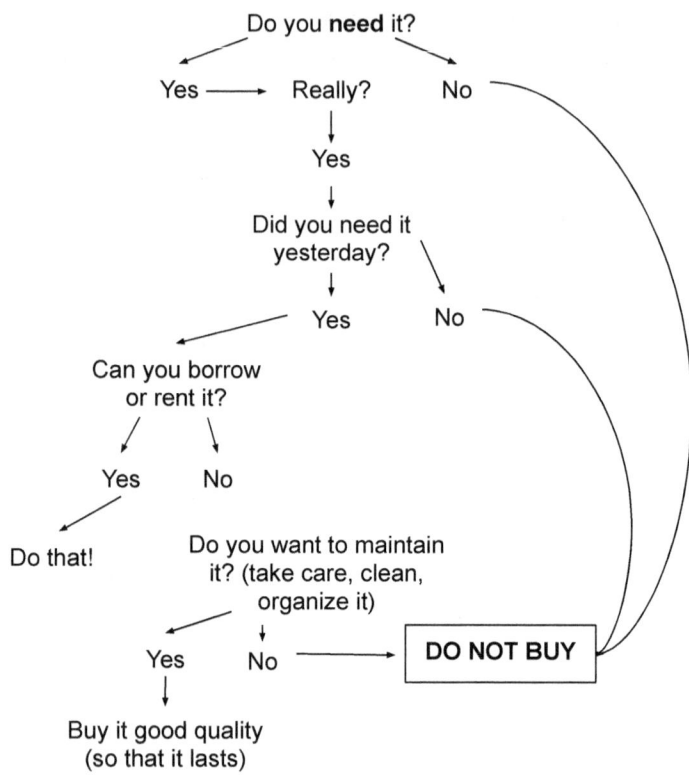

TAKEAWAYS

Humans produce immense waste through the inefficient use of resources. This creates a vast array of problems including waste that then releases greenhouse gas emissions and further climate change.

This problem stems back to the fact that we do not have a "land ethic" as Aldo Leopold noted almost seventy years ago. When we see the land as a commodity instead of a living and breathing organism, we do not value it properly and, therefore, have systems in place that exploit and destroy the land.

We must start with ourselves. We must first be kinder to the land and mindful of the waste we put out into the world. The first and most important step would be to change your mentality by **being mindful of your waste.** Coming back to the beginning quote, we must learn to "walk lightly" on this beautiful Earth.

CHAPTER 4

EXPLORING FOOD AND ENERGY

We, as individuals, have more **power** than we think. In the capitalist system that we live in, consumers determine the demand, and therefore the supply, of various products. Although it may seem as if one individual does not have the power to change the total "supply" of American industry, I will demonstrate how, contrary to popular belief, an individual *can* make a difference through changing their diet and lifestyle.

POWER OF A DIET

"You have the power to change the world, simply by changing what is on your plate."[1]
—PEOPLE FOR THE ETHICAL TREATMENT OF ANIMALS

As emphasized in the previous chapter, raising animals for food uses a lot of energy and emits carbon dioxide and methane into our atmosphere. Switching to a vegan or vegetarian diet reduces one's ecological footprint, allowing you to be more compassionate to the Earth and its inhabitants.

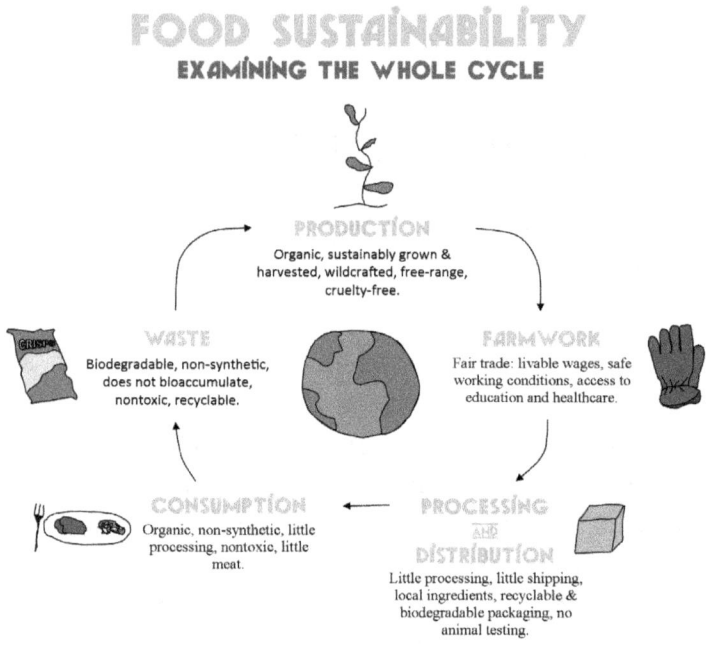

1. **Consumption**

- If a four-person family stops eating meat and cheese for one week, they reduce their environmental footprint by as much as if they stopped driving their car for thirty-five weeks.[2]
- Going one year without paper saves eight and a half trees, whereas going one year without beef saves 3,432 trees.[3]
- Livestock farming produces over 18 percent of all man-made carbon emissions.[4]

The meat and animal agriculture industry is unsustainable and one of the leading causes of deforestation and loss of biodiversity. In South America, large parts of the Amazon are clear-cut to free up space for cattle grazing. For example, in Brazil, close to 70 percent of deforestation occurs as a direct result of the increasing demand for beef.[5] As a result of this deforestation, an average of 135 plant, animal, and insect species are lost from rainforests every day.[6] It has also been estimated that the meat industry uses almost half of the land on Earth and is a leading contributor to climate change,[7] droughts, ocean dead zones, and water pollution.

As I discussed in the previous chapter, animal agriculture is one of the leading industries in the creation of pollution and waste. This results from the fact that the new age of animal agriculture production is all about volume, with factory farms crowding together hundreds of animals and feeding them antibiotics. In the United States, 99 percent of all farm animals and over forty-two million cows are raised on one of approximately 20,000 factory farms. These factory farms, or concentrated animal feeding operations (CAFOS) have been minimally regulated due to ag-gag laws that criminalize the recording of animal abuse on factory farms. This has led to a host of health and environmental problems.[8] According to the Sierra Club, this type of industrialized agriculture also undermines public health and safety.[9]

It is easy to be unaware of this information because the problems of the animal agriculture industry are hidden by the people in power. In the United States, where candidates are not forced to disclose their monetary donations, this connection between the commercial meat industry and the federal government can be hidden. Every year the meat industry donates $10.8 million to political campaigns and spends almost $7 million directly lobbying federally elected officers to avoid regulations.[10] Because of this, it is important to educate yourself about the meat industry, avoid eating as much meat, and voting for politicians who do not push unsustainable legislation.

2. Production

The various means of food production have differing degrees of impact on the environment. Eating organic foods is one of the ways to decrease the environmental impact of your food. Organic foods are foods that avoid the use of fertilizers, pesticides, growth regulators, and livestock feed additives. By eliminating artificial fertilizers and pesticides, organic farming promotes ecological balance, cycles its resources, and conserves biodiversity more effectively.[11]

Organic foods are better for the environment because they promote healthier soil and water, resulting in healthier food. Organic farming builds healthy soils by decreasing erosion, preventing water contamination, and encouraging biodiversity. Pesticides and fertilizers can run off into bodies of water causing algal blooms that can destroy entire aquatic ecosystems and water quality. Organic farming methods, including cover-crops and rotational planting, take up carbon dioxide and return it to the soil, mitigating further climate change.

Organic food is also better for you! By eating organic foods, you are avoiding toxic chemicals and highly processed foods while also supporting more sustainable farming practices.

On average, organic foods provide "a quarter more nutrients per bite than if eating produce grown with farm chemicals."[12]

3. Farmwork

The way your food is produced relies on farming methods.

- More efficient irrigation practices can also decrease the amount of water used and maximize the efficiency of agriculture. Drip and micro-sprinklers, for example, can reduce the volume of water applied to agricultural fields by 30–70 percent and can increase crop yields by 20–90 percent.[13]
    - Unfortunately, most farms do not employ efficient water usage techniques. Drip irrigation is used on less than 2 percent of irrigated land worldwide.
    - Reducing US irrigation demands by even 10 percent could free up enough freshwater to meet the new urban and industrial water demands anticipated for 2025.

4. Processing & Distribution

Where and how your food is distributed determines its sustainability. Local food, which can be found in farmers markets or from local vendors and shops, is environmentally friendly because:

- It decreases the distance your goods have to travel, which in turn decreases the emissions from the delivery vehicles.
- You know where your food is coming from—going to farmers markets allows you to interact with the producers

of the food and understand the production methods used by the farm.
- By supporting small farms, you are endorsing an industry that is closer to the land and does not exploit the land nearly as much as agricultural corporations do.

Of course, the most local "farm" is found when you grow your own food, which completely minimizes emissions. This can be as simple as putting a leftover scallion into a cup of water and letting it regrow or planting some herbs (I just planted basil, parsley, thyme, cilantro, and sage in my dorm room) instead of buying them.

POWER OF ENERGY CONSUMPTION
Our lives revolve around energy. In the modern world, practically everything needs to be powered by some sort of source. The Industrial Revolution made the economy reliant on non-renewable energy sources, but this does not have to be the case in the future.

Renewable energies—including wind, solar, geothermal, bioenergy, and hydropower energy sources—have the potential to provide more than sixteen times the current US electricity demands and using wind, solar, or geothermal could meet these needs.[15] We could use renewable energies to replace coal, revitalizing green energy industries and decreasing fossil fuel emissions.

Additionally, green energy sources are economically viable. The Union of Concerned Scientists demonstrated that a transition to renewables could save the average US household

$900 on electricity and transportation per year.[16] Transitioning to renewables as a country is not as "extreme" as people make it out to be. A study done by McKinsey & Company showed that the US could fund a low-carbon economy mostly "from investments that would otherwise have been made in traditional capital." Globally, investing $170 billion each year in energy efficiency would bring an "energy savings ramping up to $900 billion annually by 2020." Renewable energy industries could provide three times the number of jobs as coal and gas.[17]

Many countries are already moving toward becoming completely renewable.[18] Iceland, Norway, Uruguay, and Costa Rica are all almost 100 percent renewable.[19] Other countries are working toward that goal. For example, Sweden, which is 54.5 percent renewable, has pledged to reach 100 percent by 2040.[20] Countries including Germany, Monaco, Morocco, Nicaragua, China, New Zealand, and the United Kingdom are also following the same path, increasing renewable energies nationally.[21] This demonstrates the potential for renewable energy to become the norm that we can promote. In the meantime, we can do what we can to decrease our individual energy usage. Here are some tips on minimizing energy usage.[22]

1. Shut down your computer

Computers are some of the biggest energy users, so turning off your monitor at night helps save energy.

2. Choose the right light

LED bulbs are the most energy efficient lighting option and use 75 percent less electricity than incandescent bulbs.[23] They also have no mercury, which is a health hazard, and last about 25 times longer than traditional incandescent bulbs.

3. **Unplug idle electronics**

Most devices, including televisions, microwaves, scanners, and printers use standby power, even when off. In the US, the total electricity consumed by idle electronics equals the annual output of twelve power plants.[24] Use a power strip to reduce your plug load so that you can turn off all power at once.

4. **Turn off the lights**

Save energy by doing a quick "one-minute scan" before leaving your home to check if you turned off all the lights and have any appliances you can unplug.

5. **Decrease transportation energy**

Instead of driving somewhere near, try to walk or bike there. Although at first it may seem inconvenient, it is good exercise and you will feel happier that you are helping your body and your planet!

TAKEAWAYS

We can adjust our individual consumption and energy production to fit a life consistent with our environmental advocacy.

In the first half of this chapter, I emphasized that changing the food you eat is a powerful first step in becoming an eco-winner. According to environmentalist and author Frances Moore Lappé, the power of consumers and small farmers is greater than many people think. She writes, "We think we have detached ourselves from our food and its production, but food is in fact the most direct link between consumer and producer. Every man must eat, just as we need to breathe and sleep. This makes food—and even more so the way we eat—a powerful tool for permanent change."[25] I have seen this theme more and more clearly, and in a coming chapter, I will discuss eco-winner Leah Penniman, who started Fire Soul, a sustainable community farm in New York.

In the second half of this chapter, you learned that renewable energies are both economically and physically viable, and that you can also do a lot to reduce your own personal energy output. My goal was to show a different way of thinking about food and energy and for you to start to see everyday essentials as opportunities for change. Later in the book, I discuss the story of Ursula Sladek, an eco-winner who transitioned her community to renewable energy.

CHAPTER 5

WHY WE SHOULD STAY POSITIVE

―

Never doubt that a small group of thoughtful, committed citizens can change the world; indeed, it is the only thing that ever has.

—MARGARET MEAD

While reading about the world and its problems, it is easy to start to feel powerless. However, more people than ever before in history are understanding the effects of climate change and are ready to make an impact.

According to a Yale survey, 73 percent of Americans accept that climate change is happening, and over half are very sure about that fact. This is the highest this number has ever been, up from 63 percent in 2015.[1] People are understanding that climate change is real at a level they never have before. This likely means that people are more open to learning how they can help minimize its effects—you being one of those people. Perhaps what we need now is a new conversation, not about whether climate change is real, but about what we can do together to stop it.

A couple of years ago, I read *Eco Mind,* a book that inspired me to adopt a more positive outlook on the global environmental crisis. The author Frances Moore Lappé, is an influential eco-winner and the co-founder of three national organizations that explore the roots of hunger, poverty, and environmental crises.[2] Lappé argues that the main reason we are moving backward is that too many of us feel powerless. She writes that the general public feels overpowered by big companies, shut out of democracy when it comes to making a difference in the environment. She emphasizes that the worldview we absorb every day is driven by the fear of being without—a world with separation, scarcity, and stasis. This mental frame is flawed and acts as a trap that defeats us.[3]

Mindset is critical to an eco-winner. Without the proper mindset, an eco-winner cannot achieve the successful traits I talked about earlier: commitment, confidence, consistency, and creativity. The good news is that our mindsets *can* be changed by people that are promoting environmental goals. In this chapter, I will discuss the various environmental groups an eco-winner can join to make a bigger impact.

THE POWER OF GROUPS

Environmental advocacy centers around groups. By joining a group of like-minded individuals, one can become a more powerful entity that has a greater voice to advocate with.

This is because groups provide a basis for a larger volunteer and political force with more votes and influence. The most effective political intervention happens through organizations, including environmental interest groups, nonprofits, and market-based groups.

1. **Nonprofits**

Nonprofits or nongovernmental organization (NGOs) currently make up 4.2 percent of the gross domestic product (GDP), which is 77 percent higher than in 1989, illustrating the increasing size and power of these organizations. Many nonprofits, including Greenpeace, Climate Action, the Worldwide Fund for Nature (WWF), and the Third World Network have had immense impacts on global environmental politics. These groups have been **creative** in the ways in which they garner media attention. For example, one of my favorite movements was when more than 100,000 protesters from various NGOs convened, some dressed as penguins and polar bears, carrying signs saying "Save the Humans" during the UN climate change talks in 2009.[4] These activists carry the very important role of making sure that governments uphold their environmental pledges and act as "whistle blowers" when the state falls behind.

2. **Environmental Interest Groups**

Interest groups play an important role in US and global environmental legislation. Interest groups lobby for or against certain legislation, highlighting the constant power struggle between activist organizations and industry. Groups including the Sierra Club, Environmental Defense Fund,

Nature Conservancy, Natural Resources Defense Council, and American Rivers all fight for a shared agenda and have been successful.

3. Market-Based Groups

Market-based approaches have also been used to help solve environmental problems. For example, throughout the world, the trade of carbon offsets is being used to address deforestation by replanting forests. Carbon offsets are reductions in emissions of carbon dioxide or other greenhouse gases that compensate for emissions made elsewhere.[5] In Chiapas, Mexico, the carbon mitigation program Fondo Bioclimático provides extra income for subsistence farmers while also addressing climate change. In this program, public agencies fund poor communities of farmers by providing them with seeds and other resources needed to grow trees. NGOs monitor and help the process while businesses buy the carbon certifications. As a result, this single carbon forestry project helped contract over ten thousand tons of carbon dioxide.[6] The Environmental Program at the William and Flora Hewlett Foundation in California is known for its successful market-based program against climate change. The Hewlett program funds an international network of scientists, lawyers, and campaigners to bring emissions trading into American and international policy.[7]

Together, we make up the **global civil society:** the conglomerate of all the different groups engaged in shaping global environmental government processes. The global civil society is made up of a multitude of eco-winners that change the

Earth through small community efforts and legislation. That is why we should stay positive.

As seen with these examples, with groups, we can harness the power of cooperation, especially in a time when we are seeing the trend of non-state actors becoming more powerful in local and global environmental politics.

ENVIRONMENTAL ADVOCACY GROUPS
You can join three major categories of environmental groups.

1. **Mainstream Organizations**

Mainstream organizations are based in Washington DC and focus on the public policy aspect of environmentalism. Some examples include the Sierra Club and the Audubon Wildlife Association. These organizations lobby members of Congress and staff, mobilize members to contact public officials, and defend and challenge the environmental decisions of agencies.

2. **Greens Organizations**

Greens organizations emphasize the public education, direct action, and social change aspect of environmental advocacy. Whereas mainstream organizations look more toward influencing government, greens organizations are dedicated more to "eco-centric" philosophies: basic changes in human values and behavior. Some examples would include Earth First! and Greenpeace.

3. Grassroots Groups

Grassroots groups deal more with local environmental issues such as threats from hazardous waste sites, urban sprawl, or the loss of land. In the past fifteen years, there have been more than twelve thousand grassroots groups.[8]

Eco-winners from each of these groups will be discussed later on in the book. With environmental advocacy, one gets to choose the group they want to be part of the most and become an active member!

TAKEAWAYS

We should stay positive for a lot of reasons. In fact, it is a myth that the Earth's common resources cannot be sustainably managed. As mentioned by Elinor Ostrom, environmental economist and Nobel Prize winner, there have been many different examples in which communities have managed their lands sustainably for thousands of years. This destroys the notion that humans are trapped in a situation they cannot change: that it is impossible to reverse the fate of climate change.

With like-minded eco-winners working together to promote a future in which we sustainably manage our resources, we can work toward creating a greener planet. Environmental groups are powerful because they magnify their voice. Even in politics, which may seem fixed and impenetrable, environmental advocacy groups are pushing through their ideals and making an impact. As summarized by environmental specialist Kate O'Neill, "Activists make international organizations rethink the ways in which they take into account broader societal interests... through lobbying government officials, using the media and Internet, and protesting and organizing parallel summits."[9]

In these past few chapters, we learned about our eco-history. Evidently, many challenges lie ahead. In the next section, we will cover what it means to be an eco-winner and how you can join the effort to be a part of the solution.

2

ECO-WINNERS

CHAPTER 6

EXTREMISM— AN ECO-WINNER TRAIT

"The Extinction Rebellion are carrying a message we all need to hear. They won't be silenced by a police crackdown, nor should they be in a free democratic society."

—CAROLINE LUCAS, BRITISH GREEN PARTY

Many people called Thunberg an "extremist" for adamantly striking every day for climate reform, but extremism often works hand in hand with advocacy. I realized that many movement leaders were called "extremists" in their day after reading Martin Luther King Jr.'s "Letter from Birmingham Jail." King wrote that he and other leaders—like Lincoln, Jesus, Jefferson—were all characterized as extremists because they fought for the principles they believed in. The same can be said for eco-winners. People may label them as extremists and doubt their beliefs, but having a strong commitment to one's goal is a very distinct power.

When my friend told me about the Extinction Rebellion, an extremist environmental group, I decided to research and find out what made it so successful in fighting the global biodiversity loss.

THE EXTINCTION REBELLION

Currently, 40 percent of living species are at risk of going extinct; and we are looking at mass starvation in the next ten years.[1] This was the original call to action of the environmental movement called the Extinction Rebellion (XR). XR is an international movement that uses non-violent civil disobedience to fight against climate change and biodiversity loss. On their website, the XR affirms that they protest to achieve radical change and "minimize the risk of human extinction and ecological collapse."[2]

The Extinction Rebellion was established in 2018 in the United Kingdom, with one hundred academics signing a call to action in October,[3] and launching off at the end of the month by activists from the human rights group Rising Up![4] The Extinction Rebellion's three core demands include the following.

1. Telling the Truth: For the government to address the ecological crisis and declare a climate emergency.
2. Zero Emissions by 2025: For there to be no fossil fuel emissions by 2025 in the United Kingdom.

3. Citizen's Assembly: For the creation of a citizens' assembly to devise environmental policy.

The XR staged its first protest in November 2018, where thousands of activists gathered to block London bridges for climate rebellion.[5] In April 2019, the XR continued this mass protest and occupied four prominent sites in central London: the Oxford Circus, Marble Arch, Waterloo Bridge, and Parliament Square in an attempt to push natural resource and energy regulations. Even Greta Thunberg came and spoke at the 2019 XR event, showing how eco-winners continuously support each other.

In these movements, protesters would stand with posters, sing, write letters, and even get arrested. In fact, XR members are ready to do almost anything for the movement. In the 2018 and 2019 protests, some glued their hands to government buildings, thousands blocked bridges, and dozens willingly went to jail. In a documentary, one protester claimed: "I am willing to be arrested, to be jailed, and I am willing to die for this movement because I am not leaving my kids with a future that they are set on right now."[6] One XR organizer explained that "people actually want to get arrested because they want to raise the profile of their issue" and this undying commitment is what defines the movement. One protester lying in the middle of Lambeth Bridge sang, "Never doubt that a small group of people can change the world; indeed, it is the only thing that ever has."

I was touched by the tenacity of these activists. Their deep **commitment** and **confidence** in their ability to make an impact is what characterizes them as eco-winners—and as extremists.

Since the London Bridge Movement, the Extinction Rebellion has spread to all parts of the Earth, leaving a global impact. On March 22, 2019, the Extinction Rebellion in Australia held a "Declaration Day" in Melbourne, Adelaide, Sydney, and Brisbane, where demonstrators assembled and protested to demand that governments and media declare a state of climate emergency. On April 15, the eve of International Rebellion Day, an XR group occupied Australia's Parliament's Lower House[7] and even had to be forcibly removed. Meanwhile, Extinction Rebellion protests were being organized in twenty-seven other countries including Ireland, Canada, France, Sweden, Germany, Colombia, and New Zealand,[8] as well as in New York City for a national day of action.[9]

XR Protesters blockading the Waterloo Bridge in the 2019 London Protest movement[10]

THE IMPACT OF THE EXTINCTION REBELLION

The Extinction Rebellion has worked to advance their three core demands to make the Earth a greener and more just place. Although these demands have not been fully met, there has been progress that would not have occurred without the movement.

1. Telling the Truth

Partly through pressure from the Extinction Rebellion, "Scores of councils and local authorities in the UK have declared a climate emergency in recent months, as has the Labour party. Increasing numbers of politicians—certainly on the opposition benches—acknowledge that this is the biggest challenge facing humanity."[11]

2. Zero Emissions by 2025

Although the UK is nowhere near reaching this demand, the Extinction Rebellion still stirred up change. *The Guardian* acknowledged that "The fact that this demand is now out there has changed the parameters of the debate."[12] The week of the demonstrations, confronted by XR protesters outside Parliament, Labour's Diane Abbott said that members of parliament needed to come together to host a "broad conversation" about hitting net zero by 2025. Furthermore, the Committee on Climate Change decided that the UK should legislate for and reach a net-zero emissions goal by 2050, so as to end its contribution to global warming within thirty years.[13]

3. Citizens' Assembly

No sign currently exists at the moment that the government intends to set up a citizens' assembly to address the climate crisis. However, a few Labour members of Parliament—including Stella Creasy and Jon Ashworth—have backed the idea.

TAKEAWAYS

The main idea is that environmental norms are shifting. The Extinction Rebellion's mass protests have gained massive media coverage and inspired many other activists to take action around the world. The efforts and sacrifices of thousands of eco-winners *has* made a difference.

As summarized by author and XR expert Mathew Taylor,

> "The truth about the climate crisis—and the existential threat it poses to humanity—is, campaigners argue, now in the public domain and can no longer be ignored by those in power. The language around climate change has also changed. Words like 'extinction,' 'rebellion,' 'crisis,' and 'breakdown' are now part of everyday conversations when discussing the environmental threat. But perhaps most importantly what is deemed 'politically realistic' has changed. In the eyes of many seasoned observers, the past two weeks represent a "tipping point," with the Extinction Rebellion protests coinciding with more school strikes for the climate, the BBC's David Attenborough documentary, and Mark Carney telling bankers they can

no longer ignore the threat. The question now is whether politicians are prepared to rise to the challenge."¹⁴

This brings us back to the idea of extremism. In a way, extremism—when not violent—fits into the traits of eco-winners. In our case, these "extremist" advocates are really just incredibly **committed, confident, consistent,** and **creative** individuals. The logo on the Extinction Rebellion website reads, "THIS IS AN EMERGENCY." In all their movements, the XR's mindset is that we need to act now. Their extremism is a reflection of the severity of the ecological crisis, which reminds us to act.

CHAPTER 7

GRASSROOTS TO NOBEL PEACE PRIZE

―

"We are still living in denial. We are still denying who we are. We are still denying our roots. If we can recapture some of that, that the trees are important, the birds are important, then we would be able to take care of the environment. And I know if we are able to take care of the environment, we can survive."

—WANGARI MAATHAI

Maathai is the founder of the Green Belt movement—a grassroots movement that aims to organize women in Kenya to plant trees to combat deforestation, promote wellbeing, and empower women—for which she won the Nobel Peace Prize in 2004.

Every eco-winner has a source of inspiration. For Maathai, that was nature itself; specifically, a huge tree near her home in the central highlands of rural Kenya. In the *Taking Root* documentary, Maathai said, "My mother told me not to collect wood from the fig tree and when I asked 'Why?' she said because that tree is the tree of God."[1] At the time, Maathai did not understand her mother's words. When she returned to her hometown twenty years later, the tree was gone, replaced with a building. The once species-abundant stream ecosystem had disappeared, and with it, the community's water source. That was when Maathai understood the reason for the name "tree of God." The tree gave life to the environment around itself—provided water, supported species and habitats, and recycled nutrients. The interconnectedness of nature stemming from trees served as Maathai's inspiration, galvanizing her internationally known Green Belt movement.

Maathai was born in Nyeri, a rural part of Kenya. She started on her path of education after her eldest brother recommended to their mother that she attend school. Maathai stayed in school for twelve years, determined to master reading and writing. In 1960, she won a US scholarship and left Kenya to pursue biological sciences at Benedictine College and obtain a Master of Science from the University of Pittsburgh. Her five years in the States changed her perspective on what it meant to be respected and a good citizen.

After coming back to Kenya, Maathai was reminded that "being an African woman, there were certain things she could not do and certain goals she could not obtain."[2] However, Maathai did not let gender barriers stop her. She went on to eventually pursue doctoral studies in Germany and at the

University of Nairobi, where she became the first woman in East and Central Africa to earn a doctoral degree.

Only after all of this time did Maathai return to her hometown and see the power of nature's vast interconnectedness through the relationship between the fig tree and the stream. As rain falls, the tree's roots fix the soil, increasing water absorption. The water then percolates into underground reservoirs, which then feed into streams and other bodies of water. People are unaware of how much they depend on the survival of ecosystems, but this relationship is especially emphasized in small communities like Nyeri. An unhealthy ecosystem can deprive these communities of their resources through water drainage and deforestation.

Maathai's experiences reminded me of the importance of *ecosystem services*, the benefits that natural systems provide to society and the environment. Though it is common knowledge that trees regulate carbon dioxide levels and provide habitats for species, they also maintain a stable water supply.

Every ecosystem has its own unique services. Wetlands filter and purify the surface water, prevent flooding, and serve as habitats for migratory birds.[3] Coral ecosystems serve as a habitat and source of food for millions of diverse and rare species, protect coastlines from storms and erosion, and provide jobs in fishing, recreation, and tourism.[4] In other words, ecosystems are critical to both human and animal life, and like Maathai emphasizes, we tend to not understand how much we depend on them. This type of thinking leads us to overexploit these ecosystems for short-term monetary gain. "When people say they want to come in and cultivate, or they want to come in and grow plantations, I know that they are digging their own graves," Maathai summarized.

With the cutting down of trees comes the disappearance of water. In Africa, during European colonization, innumerable trees were cut down to make building materials and space for farming cash crops like coffee and tea. Because of this conversion, rural communities did not have enough firewood to cook their original, nutrient-rich foods, and instead were forced to adopt highly-refined food diets that contained almost no vitamins and proteins. The children that subsisted on these diets suffered from malnutrition. The root of the problem, deforestation, led to desertification and increased the struggle for rural communities to obtain necessary nutrients and water.

Maathai understood that to return the land to its previous harmonious state, she would have to bring back the trees.

THE FOUNDING OF THE GREEN BELT MOVEMENT

In 1972, Maathai began laying the foundations for the Green Belt movement. The movement started as a campaign to solely plant trees. Maathai traveled to various villages in Kenya and gathered the women at community meetings to explain the relationship between desertification and trees. After these meetings, Maathai planted trees with the women. As she moved on to the next community, the women were incentivized to continue planting trees because Maathai offered them four cents per seedling planted. This strategy encouraged women in other communities to join the movement. These women also started planting native crops instead of cash crops. As time went on, the planting communities started noticing that their children were growing healthier and required less medicine. The children now ate a variety of native foods. One Kenyan woman recalled, "If I were still planting old crops, I would not look this good. My friends look older."

A MOVEMENT IN A TIME OF POLITICAL INSTABILITY

At the time, the political climate of Eastern Africa was democratically unstable. This instability started with the British arriving in East Africa in the 1880s. At the time, there were over forty indigenous nations living in present-day Kenya. However, with imperialism, many of the indigenous peoples were killed and had their huts burned down. In place of the natural landscape of forests, the colonists built roads, settlements, and plantations. Most native African people were relocated to larger villages that were created through massive deforestation and the anti-colonial groups that remained—like the Mau Mau—sought refuge in the forest, but were bombed.[5] The remaining groups were forced to assimilate and the traditional African values of conserving nature were lost.

In 1963, Kenya achieved independence and Jomo Kenyatta was inaugurated as Kenya's first prime minister. After his fifteen-year rule, he was succeeded by Daniel Arap Moi. Even this new autonomous Kenyan government continued to "exploit resources and enrich themselves at the expense of the environment,"[6] Maathai explained in an interview. They continued to strip forests for their resources and land and used fear tactics to prevent any intervention from dissenters.

Initially, nobody interfered with the Green Belt Movement because they did not take the women seriously. Over the course of the following years, the government started to interfere when they realized that Maathai was inspiring women to change the social construct, by requiring the women obtain a license to convene. Maathai did not let this deter the movement. She continued to meet with women and empower them to stand up for themselves. Maathai preached to the women:

"We are planting trees for our country, a legacy for our children as our ancestors left a legacy for us. So let us not be pushed around. If the Chief comes around and asks, 'Don't plant,' ask him why not. He'll say, 'Oh so you want to be rude?' Answer him. 'Trees? What's wrong with them?' Trees don't vote. Just plant them. Once you have self-knowledge, move with the wisdom of the serpent, and with the gentleness of a dove."

The Green Belt Movement became a campaign for new ideas. It gave women a reason to stand up for themselves—reasons why they should protect both their environmental and human rights. With the planting of trees, women could provide food and timber for their family.

Since 1977, the women of the Green Belt movement have planted over fifty-one million trees.[7]

As Maathai put it, *"You cannot protect the environment unless you empower people, you inform them, and make them understand that the resources are their own resources, and they must protect them."*

FACING CHALLENGES ON HER JOURNEY

Throughout her life as an eco-winner, Maathai faced even greater trials that tried to defeat her.

In 1982, the Moi leadership started a project to privatize the only public park in Nairobi and build a 60-floor skyscraper in its place, funded in part by other countries. After discovering this plan, Maathai wrote a letter to the leaders of the funding countries, arguing that they did not privatize their own parks—such as the Central Park in New York city or the Hyde Park in London—and were supporting and doing business with a dictator. Once news of these letters spread, Maathai was crudely condemned by the entire Kenyan Parliament because she disobeyed the tyrannical system at a time when disobedience was not tolerated. She became a symbol of national humiliation, and practically all of Maathai's old friends, family, and supporters chose not to associate with her any longer. Maathai recalls this challenging time in her life, and how she had to "raise [her] consciousness to a level where you feel that you must do the right thing—because the right thing is the only right thing to do." Her mindset and clear goals allowed her to push through the hate and alienation.

In the end, the international committee withdrew their funding and the private project died. This decision marked a turning point in Kenya: Maathai proved that a woman from a rural community could change the fate of an entire country.

Her list of achievements does not stop there. Throughout the years, whenever the government denied the basic rights of citizens, Maathai kept the light of rebellion burning as she stepped up and fought for democracy.

In the 1980s, she protested the unjust imprisonment of political activists with the prisoners' mothers.[8] At first, they stood outside of the parliament alone. But soon enough, more people began to join their movements, including men who had been wrongly convicted by the government. After the second day of protesting, the police shot at the protesters. In retaliation, the women—led by Maathai—stripped naked to show that they are the mothers of everyone (according to African tradition). In response, the women were badly beaten by police, and Maathai fell into a coma. Though the protest was shut down, the women, inspired by Maathai's courage, started going to the city cathedral where they educated the public of the torture endured by Kenyans and the need for democracy. These women took refuge at the cathedral for eleven months during which they continued to demand the return of their sons. The continuous pressure forced Moi to release the political prisoners.

In 1998, the Moi government planned to privatize large tracks of public land in the Karura Forest. However, Maathai was ready to fight. She sent letters to political officers, addressed the government through the press, and came to Karura Forest to plant trees and protest the forest's destruction.[9] While continuing with her tree-planting campaign, she was denied entry into the forest by a large group of men and police. But with the support she had garnered through previous efforts, large numbers of Kenyans joined her in protest. Soon, Maathai's protests against this deforestation grew to become a national movement in which the women, students, and the general public protested to save the forests. The movement expanded to advocate for political freedom, and people were less afraid to demand for a fair government. After a year of staunch protests with blood shed by protesters during rallies, all construction in the Karura Forest was stopped.

For more than thirty years, Maathai has **consistently** fought for environmental and human rights in Kenya. In 2004, Wangari Maathai was awarded the Nobel Peace Prize for her courageous efforts to protect and heal the Earth.[10]

Maathai protesting at the entrance to the Karura Forest[11]

TAKEAWAYS

One village woman stated, "Wangari has given me the strength to know if I fight for something, I can make it happen. Two options: I do it, or I die."

Maathai has no limit to what she can do. She inspired generations of Kenyans to fight for their rights, and she altered the course of history. Her nonviolent, educational, and incentivizing approach inspired women to continue to plant trees;

mothers and students to protest; and mindsets to shift, even with intervention from the government. Maathai used the power of nature to help communities. Instead of simply providing food or water to those in need, she helped them **learn** how to cultivate their own food. She pushed her advocacy until the end, even when her own life was threatened. She was always willing to fight for her goals—making her one of the most impactful eco-winners in history.

CHAPTER 8

THE IMPACT OF A STUDENT

"But in terms of how I think about the environment now, which is really different—it's much bigger than plants and animals, it's about people, it's about movements, it's about politics."

—MAY BOEVE

What kind of impact can a student really have? When one thinks of a college student, they might envision an overworked, and underpaid employee at their local coffee shop. With so much on their plates, it may seem as if they have no time for anything, much less advocacy. But what can this group do to help change the world?

To show the impact a college student can make, let's focus on eco-winner May Boeve, the executive director of 350.org, one of the most influential environmental advocacy organizations in the United States.

FROM COLLEGE TO ECO-WINNER

May Boeve, now thirty-five years old, has been an environmentalist since she was young, passionate about advocating for human, animal, and environmental rights. Boeve recalls, "I was one of those kids who ran lemonade stands to raise money for the animal rights group PETA on the weekends. I was really into activism, and I still am."[1] Boeve attended Middlebury College in Vermont, where she and some friends started to take on bigger projects.

Moving past lemonade stands, Boeve and her friends decided that they wanted to move outside the already environmentally conscious Vermont to a new state more in need of environmental activism. They decided on Montana, which had an extensive coal mining industry that could be replaced by wind power. However, just before they left, Bill McKibben, famous environmentalist and author, asked them for their help to start the environmental organization called 350.org. The organization gets its name from what some scientists say is the maximum level of carbon dioxide in the atmosphere to maintain a climate similar to the one we know today—350 parts per million (ppm). Currently, the Earth's atmosphere is over 412 ppm, according to the National Oceanic and Atmospheric Administration.[2] The point of 350.org was to organize environmental advocacy projects to help end the use of fossil fuels, transition to renewable energy, and build a global grassroots movement.[3]

Back in 2007, Boeve decided she would have more impact by accepting McKibben's offer instead of moving to Montana. Fresh out of college, but eager to make an impact, she took on the responsibility of overseeing 350.org's operations in North America. At this point, the organization was focused on organizing the 2008 Global Climate Strike, the first of its prominence. Since then, 350.org has led worldwide days of action around climate change, jump-started the campus fossil fuel divestment movement, and organized protests against the construction of pipelines.[4] In 2009, Boeve helped lead the People's Climate March in September, one of the largest climate demonstrations in history, which drew over four hundred thousand people to New York and thousands of others in 161 other countries. In the course of less than a decade, 350.org has grown under Boeve's leadership into a formidable force in the environmental movement.

AN EMPHASIS ON INCLUSIVITY
Boeve believes the way to get back to 350 ppm is to create a "massive social movement" to weaken the fossil fuel industry and embrace renewable energy. This social movement is where we all come in.

The secret to Boeve's success is her strategy of diversifying the environmental movement to include everyone. As she put it, "many people feel connected to the climate change movement, and it's important for everyone who's involved, whether they're a schoolteacher in the UK or a farmer in Burundi, to see themselves in this movement. The more leaders who reflect the diversity of the movement, the broader, the bigger, the stronger the movement will be."

350.org, under the leadership of Boeve, took the big-tent approach to the 2009 International Day of Climate Action, inviting people to join climate change demonstrations or create their own.[5] That day encouraged people not previously associated with the movement to join. New members included churches, performance artists, extreme athletes, and even Chinese businessmen holding a black-tie gala in Shanghai, unexpected, but critical, partners for 350.org due to their corporate influence.[6]

When I think of an environmentalist, I tend to assume an image—a middle-class, liberal-minded individual. This image limits the scope of groups I reach out to for demonstrations, limiting overall impact. Boeve challenges that notion, inviting people from every geographic, religious, financial, and racial background to maximize her impact. Boeve's movement is "particularly trying to undue the wrongs of the past in terms of groups that have always been excluded—people of color, women, low-income communities, queer communities" and "building this much more vibrant community that we all want to be part of and that we know is needed in this country." In your own advocacy, **do not count anyone out.** Talk to everyone—you never know who you will inspire. When I shared the environmental effects of eating meat with my family, I was incredibly surprised that my parents became pescatarian. Even my brother, the meat lover of the family, seriously decreased his intake. Remember, you can have the most impact on those around you.

Learning about Boeve inspired me to interview an activist from 350.org to understand the organization on an individual level. I set out to find an eco-winner to interview for my book and sent LinkedIn messages to all the 350.org members and employees that I could find. After a couple of days, Julia Fritz-Endres, a fresh-out-of-college intern, responded. I was stoked to talk to her because, as a young student activist, I wanted to find out more about what students could do to make a difference.

After weeks of back-and-forth planning, it was proving hard to find a time to connect. In an act of spontaneity, I grabbed my phone and decided to call Fritz-Endres. To my astonishment, she picked up, and I blindly (with none of my questions prepared or my recorder set up) started my interview. Sitting on a cold bench in front of a cafe, I sat and ferociously typed her words into my phone. The interview lasted only twenty minutes... and it was one of the best interviews I'd ever had.

YOUNG AND FEARLESS IN 350.ORG

Julia Fritz-Endres grew up in a Massachusetts historic house surrounded by nature. She went to St. Paul, Minnesota as an undergraduate, where she majored in environmental studies and focused on climate science policy. Even though the environmental field can be discouraging in the sense that so many problems need to be addressed—environmental injustice, climate change, pollution, saving animals—she knew that she wanted to work in the environmental sector.

As a junior, Fritz-Endres studied abroad in Cape Town, South Africa. There, she explored issues related to the water crisis and spent a lot of time researching and interviewing locals, trying to understand the values that shape our water consumption and usage. In Cape Town, she learned that various factors shape our environment but, despite their complexity, we "cannot just wait around and not do something."

Inspired by her experiences, Fritz-Endres wanted to do something in her own community. She applied and was accepted as an intern working with a local 350.org pipeline resistance team, which recruited many students from her college. This reinforced the idea that an **inspired student workforce,** one of Boeve's vision, is key to 350.org's success. Working at 350.org made her "feel like [she] was part of a greater thing, something tangible, hands on, that connects you to someone that is similarly minded."

For her 350.org chapter, Fritz-Endres and her team did everything in their power to stop the pipeline that was proposed by the Canadian company Enbridge to the Minnesota Public Utility Commission (PUC). The proposed pipeline project would stretch from Minnesota to Lake Superior and that summer, the PUC was going to vote on the project, five years after Enbridge announced it. Fritz-Endres's team had "no specific agenda" and instead was ready to fight as a unified force for the protection of forests and aquatic environments that would be disrupted by the pipeline.

Every day of the PUC hearings, Fritz-Endres and her team would get in line at 5 a.m., attend the day's hearing, and fight against the lobbyists Enbridge had hired. At the time, Enbridge spent over $11 million on lobbying efforts to push the Minnesota pipeline project forward.[7] This sum pales in comparison to the billions of dollars in profit the company would make from the pipeline project.

Pipeline companies like Enbridge are focused on getting permits from the Federal Energy Regulatory Commission, which authorizes them to adjust their rates on transporting gas. However, as expert Elizabeth Payne clearly put it, "While the corporations stand to benefit from tax breaks and are assured a profit, the environmental and safety risks of the pipelines will be absorbed by the communities they pass through and by everyone affected by the rapidly changing climate."[8]

Although the team fought the pipeline for a month, the PUC still granted the certificate of building to Enbridge. Though Fritz-Endres was devastated with the result, she did not lose hope. Instead, she asked herself what she should do now. As eco-winners, she and her team were not willing to step down. Her supervisor, Annie Pierson, suggested that they go up north to the Wisconsin-Minnesota border on June 29, 2018, to blockade and directly protest the construction of the Keystone XL pipeline.

Along with other environmentalists and famous indigenous activist Winona LaDuke,[10] they stood on the highway where pipeline construction was rumored to take place. They held signs in support of the rare aquatic ecosystems and marshes of Minnesota that the pipeline would likely spill crude oil into. Fritz-Endres told me as she stood on the freeway, waving her sign and singing about saving the Earth, she felt the incredible unity and power of the movement. "Seeing Winona LaDuke speak made me realize how important the movement was, and how collectively we were so **powerful**."

During our interview, Fritz-Endres said something that stuck with me:

"What you do is not always going to do something, but that does not mean it is not worth doing."

Fritz-Endres and other eco-winners are consistently living in accordance with their beliefs and moral code. An eco-winner that wants to save the environment starts with themselves, keeps fighting, and does not give up because that is their way of life: **living parallel to their goals.**

That idea became a breakthrough for me, and a wake-up call. If I truly wanted to contribute to this movement, I better start acting like it. No more single-use Starbucks straws, Saturday morning snooze buttons, or indulgent In-and-Out burgers were going to sway my commitment to a plastic-free, weekend cleanup, vegetarian life. If I truly believed in my goal, and wrote about it, it was time for me to live up to my word.

In October 2018, while I was busy applying to colleges and finishing up my last year of high school, Fritz-Endres flew out to Washington, DC, and did a sit-in at Nancy Pelosi's office calling for congressional action on climate change.[11] She, along with 150 other youth activists, got arrested for the demonstration. I was pretty surprised when Fritz-Endres told me that she was okay with being arrested. She explained that arrests act as an activist strategy in which an increase in arrests lead to greater media attention and impact. While demonstrating, she felt as if she was "part of something bigger—race, gender, age, nothing matters except your collective goal." It is a powerful concept, the idea of taking ownership of the world, speaking out against what you believe is wrong.

When I first learned about the Extinction Rebellion protesters who were willing to be arrested, their commitment seemed noble, but extreme, something I would never do. Talking to Fritz-Endres made me realize that powerful and influential eco-winners are really not that different from me.

Julia Fritz-Endres and May Boeve inspired me. They never gave up, connected across space and time by the eco-winner traits that are crucial to the ongoing success of present and future environmental leaders.

1. **Commitment:** They had a steady commitment toward their goal of stopping the pipeline, and they were passionate enough to devote time toward realizing their goal.
2. **Confidence:** They were confident that what they are doing, coming to the public utility commission hearings to argue against the project, and demonstrating on highways against the pipeline, works and could potentially stop the building of the pipeline.
3. **Consistency:** These people had grit and they are consistently fighting for what they believe in, not giving up even if they failed the first time. This tenacity is what makes them so successful because if they lose on one angle, they come about it from another way.
4. **Creativity:** Creativity makes advocacy possible. All advocacy is different and specific to the area and goal it is trying to achieve, which is why advocates must be flexible to take various steps in achieving their goal. In this case, the advocates that fought to oppose the XL Pipeline first tried

as hard as they could to stop the PUC from giving the permit of construction to the project, but when that failed, they immediately transitioned to fighting the actual construction with highway blockades. On top of that, they kept sending letters to government officials about the detrimental effects of the project. They harnessed creativity along with consistency to achieve their goals.

Boeve being arrested at the Keystone XL pipeline protest[12]

TAKEAWAYS

Student activists can have a large impact on the world around them. If we tap into this potential and power by committing to the movement, we can have a large influence over projects, institutions, and governments.

The stories of Boeve and Fritz-Endres prove the importance of fighting for your goals. **The notion that people, especially students, cannot create change is no longer a valid excuse.**

As an individual begins living up to their potential, more opportunities to make a difference will open up. After accepting McKibben's offer to start 350.org, Boeve organized the first global climate strike. After Fritz-Endres worked with 350.org, she traveled to Washington, DC to advocate for the environment. Surrounding myself with eco-winners and the impact of their work has pushed me to live a life filled with passion and meaning.

CHAPTER 9

FIXING THE BROKEN FOOD SYSTEM ONE FARM AT A TIME

―

"Food really can be medicine, or it can be a weapon that prevents civic participation."

—LEAH PENNIMAN

Leah Penniman, the founder of community Soul Fire Farm, summarized the flaws of the current US food system with the statement: "The food system is not broken, it is simply working as it was designed." The current system of industrialized agriculture is composed of monoculture fields dependent on chemical pesticides and fertilizer usage.[1]

Industrial farming was shaped in the 1950s and 60s through the Green Revolution, which introduced high-yielding varieties of seeds, increased use of fertilizers and pesticides, and new irrigation methods.[2] At the time, the Green Revolution was considered a technological miracle with great implications for solving starvation all around the world.[3] However, the current system has a variety of environmental and public consequences, including contaminated soil, water, and air, a decrease in insect and organism biodiversity, and health detriments to farmers and consumers.

The issue of pesticide and fertilizer usage is shaped by government and corporate interests. US federal subsidies fund large agricultural corporations and their subsequent unsustainable farming practices, especially in the corn, soy, wheat, cotton, and rice industries.[4] Experts Anne Weir Schechinger and Craig Cox claim that "the federal crop insurance program may be encouraging farmers to plant crops that aren't drought resistant"[6] and AEI scholars note that subsidies encourage farmers "to expand crop production on highly erodible land."[7] With federal subsidies, lands that had been originally untouched or used for pasture, shift into crop production, degrading land even further.

But the most pertinent issue at hand is that federal subsidies "induce excessive use of fertilizers and pesticides."[8] The farmers of marginal lands attempt to compromise their poorer soil and climate conditions with increased fertilizers and pesticides use. These toxic chemicals run off into nearby bodies of water, resulting in water contamination. In the 1940s, the federally subsidized expansion of sugar cane production increased use of phosphorus fertilizer causing "extensive damage to the Everglades."[9]

Because subsidies are crop specific, they have discouraged crop rotation and instead promoted monoculture, which uses more fertilizers. Researcher Josh Sewell writes "the boom in corn production driven by subsidies and the ethanol mandate is generating pollution problems in the Mississippi River and the Gulf of Mexico."[10] Pollution then contaminates air, water, and soil contributing to respiratory illnesses like asthma.

To promote sustainable agriculture, change has to be enacted on both federal and community levels. The policy changes would include a ban on pesticide and fertilizer usage and the transition to sustainable and organic farming. The general public would benefit from a cleaner environment and a less toxic food supply, and farmers would benefit from safer working conditions.[11] The overall problem should be addressed through the reconsideration of subsidies in agriculture and an emphasis on more small-scale, sustainable farms.

The federal government spends more than $20 billion a year for farm businesses in total, of which approximately only 39 percent of the nation's 2.1 million farms receive subsidies.[5]

SOUL FIRE FARM
In 2006, Penniman and her husband created Soul Fire Farm, an eighty-acre organic community farm in upstate New York.[12] Soul Fire Farm sequesters approximately four thousand pounds of carbon per year, has increased topsoil depth by 300 percent, and feeds over 350 people weekly.[13] Penniman's main vision is to return to her roots, growing food to free herself and her community from depending on the industrial food complex.

During my freshman year, I had the privilege of meeting with Penniman when she visited Dartmouth College. I asked how she achieved such success, she responded that a successful project requires someone that will take care of it "as if it were their baby." It is this unwavering commitment for the project that allows it to thrive.

Penniman first began her environmental activism when her newborn daughter was exposed to lead poisoning. She and her husband then tested all of the soils in Wooster, Massachusetts, and began to push for a remediation program.

In 2006, Penniman started her Soul Fire community farm project after she and her husband bought a tract of land on the South end of Albany. They worked there for four years to convert the infertile land to be suitable for farming. It was a work-heavy project, especially because everything in the farm was built by hand. "We dug the foundation for months only to have to re-dig it after discovering that we had dug the wrong foundation," recalls Penniman. When the land was ready for cultivation, she started farming using various sustainable methods of permaculture, drawing inspiration from indigenous people. She employed techniques such as composting with worms from the time of Cleopatra, raised beds from South American indigenous peoples,[13] polycultures from Africa, and revolving legumes from North American tribes.[14] Penniman stressed the idea that sustainable farming is about cultivating land like the indigenous did, and treating the land not as a commodity, but as a "living, breathing organism." This contrasts the large-scale, monoculture, and pesticide and fertilizer-heavy agricultural system of the United States.

Soul Fire Farm also currently supports sustainable farming initiatives outside of the United States, including sibling farms in Mexico and Haiti. Soul Fire volunteers have planted over 1,500 trees in Haiti, have implemented over seventy-five composting systems, and have reconstructed 20 farms after the hurricane.[15]

Penniman represents the four C-traits:

1. **Committed,** working her land tirelessly.
2. **Confident** that she could make a difference in her community by providing food in a sustainable way.
3. **Consistently** doing something, from testing soils for lead poisoning to donating sustainably grown food to those in need.
4. **Creative** in her environmental projects, drawing inspiration from indigenous people and other innovators.

Penniman tilling the soil at Soul Fire Farm[16]

TAKEAWAYS

Though the agricultural sector has a long way until it is sustainable, eco-winners like Leah Penniman already provide green opportunities for consumers.

These small, sustainable community farms are growing in size and provide hope for a future agricultural system based solely on sustainable methods. With growing demands for sustainably sourced produce and knowledge of the harms of pesticides and fertilizers, we can help the United States shift away from industrial agriculture by sourcing sustainable food locally and supporting politicians with environmentally friendly agendas.

CHAPTER 10

WORKING FROM THE INSIDE

"Whatever issues inspire us, knowledge is not enough. Because knowledge without action, is meaningless."

—HEIDI HARMON

Turn **advocacy** into **action.**

That was the first thing Heidi Harmon, the mayor of San Luis Obispo, said to me during our interview.

Heidi Harmon was the first person I secured for an interview. When I first opened her response to my LinkedIn message, I felt as if I had won the lottery. The mayor of San Luis Obispo and champion of environmental advocacy had responded with enthusiasm when nobody else had. Then, after weeks of messaging and scheduling times to talk, I finally got ahold of Harmon for a fifteen-minute phone call. As this was my first real interview, I started with asking Heidi the broadest question I mustered up in the ten minutes before the interview: "What was your journey?" to which Heidi responded, "Did you watch my TED Talk?"

Months later, after having researched and written a large part of my book, I came back to my notes on this interview. First things first, I *had* to watch the TED Talk.

In her TED Talk titled "How to Turn Advocacy into Action," Harmon unveiled a completely different perspective, one that saw this time of crisis as an "unprecedented opportunity." Her optimism reminded me of the forward-looking mentality of other eco-winners including Thunberg and Boeve. They find opportunities for action in the most adverse of circumstances. All these eco-winners perceive climate change, deforestation, and other environmental problems as catalysts for social movements. "If we treat climate change as the true planetary emergency that it is, it will be a galvanizing force for humanity," Harmon declared in her speech. "A force that puts the long-term success of all of us over the short-term economic gains of a very few of us, a force that will inspire all of us to be engaged, no matter our differences."[1]

Harmon attended Cal Poly San Luis Obispo. Soon after that, she got married and had two children. To provide for her new family, Harmon worked tirelessly as a cleaner and invested the rest of her time in her children. Becoming a new mother brought the realization that she wanted to make the world a better place for her children. According to Harmon, the "best way to create a better world is by creating better people." The turning point for her advocacy came when Harmon watched Al Gore's documentary *The Inconvenient Truth*, after which she realized that both the lives of her own and every child were threatened by climate change. It was then that Harmon decided she had to *do* something to mitigate climate change. She summarized her efforts with the statement: "Whatever issues inspire us, knowledge is not enough. Because knowledge without action is meaningless."

What I found so incredible in Harmon's journey is that in the beginning of her advocacy, she was waiting for someone to take the lead so she could follow them. However, when nobody took the lead, she realized that *she* could be that leader. What she lacked in experience, she made up for in **courage.**

THE POWER OF COURAGE

Passion for one's goal—in our case to protect the Earth—can translate into courage and true confidence that transcends boundaries. Passion is transformative—with it, fear melts away. With this passion, you can overcome any lack of experience or magnitude of risk to do the thing you cannot *not* do.

Courage is central to environmental advocacy, and it is what distinguishes eco-winners from other people that also love and want to have an impact on this Earth. An eco-winner is **willing to take risks.** Greta Thunberg was willing to skip school for a one-person strike, even though it seemed that nothing could come from it. Julia Butterfly Hill, an activist that fought against deforestation in the US, was willing to spend over two years high in the branches of a redwood to protect it from being cut down, an action that seems irrational and insane. Wangari Maathai was willing to spend decades planting trees in various communities although she was ostracized, beaten, and arrested. Heidi Harmon was willing to run for mayor twice even though the odds were stacked against her: a single mom who worked as a cleaner running against a business magnate with copious campaign funds. Courage is one of the traits that all eco-winners share.

Mayor Harmon shared with me that she used to be afraid to speak in front of audiences, something that is hard to believe considering her effortless public presence. When I asked her how she conquered her fears, she said that "the important thing for all of us is not to get it right, it's not to win, it's to **begin.** Begin exactly how we are and where we are."

STEPPING UP TO TAKE ACTION
Harmon started small, first joining people and organizations with the same beliefs. However, she felt as if she could do more. She got more deeply involved and took on leadership positions in those organizations. In particular, she is chair of the Climate Change Task Force of the Santa Lucia Chapter of the Sierra Club, Program Director of the SLO Chapter of 350.org, and serves as Outreach Ambassador for the San Luis Obispo Chapter of the Citizens Climate Lobby.[2]

As she ventured into the world of environmental advocacy, volunteering, and attempting to persuade governments to adopt environmentally friendly agendas, she realized that instead of being on the outside demanding the right thing, she could be on the inside, *doing* the right thing. "Activists spend a lot of time outside the halls of power hoping that those inside make the right decisions."[3]

It is not enough to march on the streets. We need to march into our school boards and city halls and into Congress to make the changes we really need. We need elected officials that care more about the next generation than they do about the next election. With this realization, Harmon decided to fully embrace her potential to lead and ran for mayor. During this first campaign, Harmon ran against an oil magnate. By the end of her campaign against him, he was advocating for renewable energy. She lost, but for her, it was still a victory.

In 2016, Harmon met Bernie Sanders, one of her greatest political role models. He advised her, saying, "Don't get mad, go home and run for office." Harmon did exactly that. Instead of giving up, she decided to once again run for office. With a small campaign and almost no political experience, she was elected mayor by forty-six votes. Heidi Harmon has been the mayor of San Luis Obispo ever since, and she has never stopped advocating for green politics.

She told me that many of the environmental projects she had been fighting for prior to being elected, are now being brought to life by the city. In 2018, Harmon helped pass San Luis Obispo's 2035 carbon neutrality target to become a city that creates as much renewable energy as it takes to support all life there. This ambitious target is set ten years ahead of California's statewide goal.[4] In 2019, Harmon also updated bicycle safety policies[5] and pushed through energy policies that pave the way for new all-electric buildings.[6] Harmon believes that "the future of the planet depends on climate action, and San Luis Obispo's decision sets a worldwide example."[7] San Luis Obispo's political engagement is at an all-time high. "It is in the everyday moments that we need to stand up. In such a time like this, we need to step up and be active allies, not bystanders."

By taking an active stance in their communities, eco-winners are the visionaries we need.

We must show up—whether that means showing up to a march, council meeting, or even to run for office. The age, gender, or level of experience does not matter because our potential does not hinge on what we already know. Instead, our potential hinges on **what we are willing to do.** If something speaks to you so deeply that you must act, then **act.** Do the thing you cannot not do.

This is how you make the impossible, the inevitable.

Heidi Harmon in her reelection campaign[8]

Students and activists can become politically engaged in so many ways. One of the first steps is to go out and **vote**.

The good news is that young people have been doing exactly that. As a result, younger generations have had more of an impact on elections in recent years. Specifically, in the 2018 midterm elections, roughly 31 percent of youth (ages eighteen to twenty-nine) turned out to vote, an extraordinary increase from 2014, when approximately 21 percent of eligible young voters went to the polls.[9] It is estimated that this is by far the highest level of participation among youth in the past quarter century. Furthermore, the youth turnout demonstrates the willingness of young people to take responsibility for the world they are going to inherit. From the gun control movement after the Parkland shooting[10] to increased voter registration,[11] the youth has demonstrated newfound levels of engagement and enthusiasm. The rise in youth's voter turnout has also created a powerful voting bloc in favor of more liberal Democratic candidates that usually have more environmentally friendly agendas.

In addition, in several statewide races, the youth vote in the 2018 election proved to have been decisive. For example, in Wisconsin, Democratic candidate Tony Evers beat incumbent Republican Scott Walker by 1.2 percentage points, and under-thirty-year-old voters supported Evers by a twenty-three-point margin, 60 percent to 37 percent. In Nevada, where young people made up a particularly high share of the electorate that year, both the Democratic Senate candidate, Jacky Rosen, and the Democratic Governor candidate, Steve Sisolak, were projected to have won close races by less than five percentage points. In Montana, where youth made up an above-average 15 percent of the electorate, youth-supported Democrat Jon Tester won an extremely close race.[12] These results demonstrate changing norms. The youth is turning the tide of politics through their votes, a testament to the importance of political engagement.

*PRO-TIP: I recommend using environmental NGOs guides to find environmentally minded politicians and voting accordingly.

As an eco-winner, you can be creative and influence politics through more than just voting. You can support various nongovernmental organizations that lobby for the environment—such as the Sierra Club, Natural Resources Defense Council, and the Environmental Defense Fund—and contact your representatives directly through letters or calls and advocate for green legislation.

During my junior year of high school, I reached out to my local city council, asking to arrange a meeting to talk about green initiatives. Through these efforts, I was connected with Los Angeles councilmember Mike Bonin and the Deputy Chief of Staff Krista Kline. When I came into the office, they listened to my ideas on how to make Los Angeles greener. It just happened that at the time, they were trying to pass urban forestry legislation, but needed evidence of support from residents. So, I offered to help spread a survey on the likes of urban forestry, connecting residents with green government legislation.

With this situation, I came to understand that I could make a disproportionately large impact if I collaborated with the government. So, that same year, I interned for environmentally conscious Assemblyman Jesse Gabriel. Every day I came into the office, I actively proposed green measures and offered to stay in longer to work on green projects including identifying locations for clean-ups and volunteer work in Los Angeles. Through all of my volunteer work, I learned that I could make the biggest impact by collaborating with my community and partnering with my government.

TAKEAWAYS

By staying active and taking small steps, we can build a movement.

As Harmon stated in her TED Talk, "While we are building this movement, this movement is building us." By following our passion and building a movement, we can make a difference. We can use politics as a way to influence the world and push through greener ideals. While we are pushing through these ideals in voting or advocating, we grow—just as Heidi grew to be a leader in the political sphere, and how she grew to be courageous enough to run for office. Or how I grew as an individual after I first came to speak to the council. *This is the power of an eco-winner.*

CHAPTER 11

SUPPORTING ECO-WINNERS

―

"Nobody achieves anything great because they are happy and lazy."

—ALEX HONNOLD

How can one create a powerful environmental advocacy project if they do not devote their entire career to it?

I was asking myself this question when researching for my book one Sunday night, when my parents asked me to join them for movie night. They were watching the National Geographic documentary *Free Solo* about the American rock climber Alex Honnold. The movie detailed the first ever free-solo climb of El Capitan peak in Yosemite.

A couple of weeks later, I opened the list of eco-winners that I planned to research almost half a year prior. As I went through the list of potential environmentalists to write about,

I was surprised to see Alex Honnold on my sheet. How did a professional climber also end up on a list of great environmental advocates?

FROM CLIMBER TO ECO-WINNER

Honnold grew up in Sacramento, California, with his parents and sister. His mother, Diedre Wolownick, was a French teacher and his father, Charles Honnold, was a traveling enthusiast and the main supporter of his son's rock climbing.[1] Honnold started climbing at the age of five and by his teenage years, he was participating in many national youth climbing championships.[2]

He started school at the University of California, Berkeley to study civil engineering, but during his first year of college, he dropped out after his father died from a heart attack.[4] Instead of returning to college, Honnold spent most of his time living in a minivan and climbing throughout California.[5] In the following years, Honnold continued to free solo various peaks, gaining more popularity.[6] On June 3, 2017, he made his most famous climb, the first free solo ascent of El Capitan, completing the 2,900-foot route in three hours and fifty-six minutes.[7] Since then, he has continued to set more records and make a name for himself in the climbing world.

What interested me the most, however, was Honnold's philanthropy. He has always been environmentally conscious, living in his van and being vegetarian. He writes, "I'm deeply worried about the future of the world in the face of climate change, the unbridled use of fossil fuels, and so on."[8]

It was this passion that led him to establish the Honnold Foundation.

In 2012, Honnold started the foundation in an effort to help the environment and "improve people's standard of living."[9] The main focus of the foundation is to promote solar energy access all over the world. It donates money to nonprofits that work to alleviate climate change and poverty in the US, Mexico, and Africa through the implementation of solar energy. Some of these partners include GRID Alternatives, Casa Pueblo, North End Woodward Community Coalition, and Solar Energy Foundation.

1. **GRID Alternatives**

GRID Alternatives is a nonprofit that was launched in Oakland, California, by engineers Erika Mackie and Tim Sears during the 2001 California energy crisis. They introduced their Solar Affordable Housing program in the San Francisco Bay Area in 2004 and subsequently expanded to other parts of the state, installing free solar panels for low-income communities.[10] Throughout the process, GRID Alternatives built a large network of partnerships, funders, and volunteers. Since then, GRID has installed more than 9,500 photovoltaic solar electric systems worldwide, helping low-income families in the United States, Mexico, Nicaragua and Nepal save over $300 million in energy cost savings. These systems are expected to offset over 820,000 tons of greenhouse gas emissions, the equivalent to planting over seventeen million trees. GRID has also trained over 35,000 participants through their hands-on solar training program.[11]

"We are doing our part to change the world, one individual, one household, one neighborhood at a time."
—REBEKAH CASEY, DEVELOPMENT DIRECTOR

2. Casa Pueblo

Casa Pueblo was started by husband and wife, Alexis Massol and Tinti Deyá, in response to proposed open-pit mining in their small mountain town of Adjuntas, Puerto Rico. These eco-winners gathered their community members to oppose the mining and create Casa Pueblo. Since then, Casa Pueblo has expanded its focus to encompass environmental development and advocate for solar energy. The organization has since helped install solar energy panels in homes, grocery stores, restaurants, and fire stations in Adjuntas to help business owners cut costs on their energy bills.[12] After the devastation of Hurricane Maria in 2017, Casa Pueblo distributed over 15,000 solar lamps, providing electricity to charge phones and store medicine and food.

"Energy independence means sustainability for the island. It means economic activation and reducing our ecological footprint."
—ARTURO MASSOL-DEYÁ, ASSOCIATE DIRECTOR

3. North End Woodward Community Coalition

In 2007, in the North End neighborhood of Detroit, fifteen community groups came together to create the Storehouse of Hope, an organization that provided services and basic necessities for formerly incarcerated people. After noticing that the people they were supporting couldn't keep jobs because of a lack of transportation, Storehouse of Hope branched off into a new organization called the North End Woodward Community Coalition (NEWCC) to work on transit justice issues.[13]

NEWCC's work with solar energy began in 2010 in response to the city of Detroit's decision to turn off and neglect to fix streetlights in multiple neighborhoods, which left students to wait for their school buses in the dark. NEWCC raised money for solar streetlights and placed them on private land, so they wouldn't be affected by the city's ability to fix them. During the same period, NEWCC purchased fifteen homes at risk of foreclosure, placed them in Detroit's single community land trust, and installed solar panels on those homes.[14]

"The sun doesn't just shine on the rich and famous, the sun shines on all of us."

—REV. JOAN ROSS, EXECUTIVE DIRECTOR

4. Solar Energy Foundation

Solar Energy Foundation (SEF) was founded by Samson Tsegaye Lemma in 2006 with the vision of increasing the availability of solar in Ethiopia. In 2016, the Honnold Foundation "provided SEF with a grant to help Samson advance the organization through a sudden shift in governmental NGO regulations."[15] Solar Energy Foundation was the first organization in Africa to introduce "pay-as-you-go" financing for solar energy systems.[16] SEF also provides job training, product sales, and panel repairs throughout Ethiopia. Since its founding, it has trained sixty-five solar technicians, provided solar lights to 160 schools and thirty-five health centers, and sold over 30,000 solar lighting products.

Honnold used his public profile to support the projects of these eco-winners by creating his foundation, to which he donates one-third of his own profits. Honnold wrote that he wanted to fund projects that would make a difference, because many illegitimate organizations are out there. In an interview explaining his foundation, Honnold affirms that "with carbon credits, it's unclear what your money is supporting oftentimes. And I think the best carbon credit schemes are when you're supporting specific projects that improve peoples' quality of life, which is ultimately what I'm trying to do through the Honnold Foundation."[17] Honnold took what he had—money and popularity—to fight for what he cares for by supporting other organizations.

"I think the trends of human history are all in a positive direction, towards greater wealth and the sense that we have access to more opportunity, and safer, cleaner, healthier, longer lifespans."

—ALEX HONNOLD

Alex Honnold standing next to one of his projects in Central America[18]

TAKEAWAYS

Reading Honnold's story, I understand that there are many different opportunities and ways to make the world a greener and better place. You do not have to pursue an environmental discipline. In fact, you can pursue any field and still help the environment by joining organizations, volunteering, or helping to fund environmentally oriented projects.

Honnold's foundation was an integral part of making the projects of other eco-winners succeed.

Everyone has different ways to help the environmental movement. It might be direct volunteerism, or it may be donating to an organization that is good at what they do. Honnold's foundation supports these projects monetarily, and sometimes—when you are busy devoting your life to a career—that is one of the biggest impacts you can make. There is no template, no "right" advocacy path to take. Being a student, you can devote your time toward volunteer work and active participation. Being a work-heavy adult, you can fund environmental projects.

The **opportunities** are limitless.

3

ECO-WORLD

CHAPTER 12

THE POWER OF VOLUNTEERS

—

"God has cared for these trees, saved them from drought, disease, avalanches, and a thousand tempests and floods. But he cannot save them from fools."

—JOHN MUIR

The Sierra Club was founded on May 28, 1892, in San Francisco, California, by the Scottish-American preservationist John Muir. Muir founded the club with the goal of preserving forests and pristine wilderness areas including Yosemite.[1] The Sierra Club has helped establish a series of new national parks and the National Wilderness Preservation System.[2] Since then, the Sierra Club has grown to be a national environmental organization composed of hundreds of local chapters, each powered by volunteers that focus on trail work and political activism.

INTRODUCING THE SIERRA CLUB

I volunteered for the Sierra Club for over three years. Every weekend, I hiked up the Santa Monica mountains to do trail work with the Los Angeles Sierra Club chapter. During our four-hour shifts, we cleared trails, pulled out invasive South African cape ivy, and cut down any vegetation that could easily catch fire.

The Sierra Club also sends its email-list pre-written letters advocating for environmental reforms addressed to politicians. Every time I got one of these emails, I forwarded it to my congressional representatives.

Being a part of the Sierra Club made me feel that I was following through with my beliefs, taking consistent action toward protecting the environment. More importantly, the Sierra Club introduced me to other eco-winners who inspired me to realize my vision.

REPRESENTING THE SIERRA CLUB

Sridhar Gullapalli is originally from India and came to work at the University of Southern California (USC) in 1984 when he was in his twenties. He told me that his activism started with his love for hiking. When he first started working at USC, his friend asked if he wanted to go on a hike. He liked the hike so much that he continues to trek the same routes, twenty-four years later. Throughout the years, he met and joined other hikers who were part of the Sierra Club. As Sierra Club hiking became incorporated into his life, he decided that he would train to become a wilderness leader. After volunteering as a wilderness leader for twelve years,

Gullapalli transitioned to advocacy in the Sierra Club. There are three pillars to the club, Gullapalli told me.

Three Pillars of the Sierra Club

1. Outdoors and Wilderness
2. Advocacy and Political Input
3. Conservation

The first pillar centers around hiking and exploring nature. The second pillar centers around influencing an environmentally conscious agenda in the political realm, and the third pillar centers around making real change in communities through volunteer work.

In 2014, Gullapalli ran for a position on the Executive Committee for the Angeles Sierra Club chapter. The Executive Committee of the Sierra Club is the chapter's governing body, which meets weekly to make decisions on how to influence government policy. With Gullapalli's initiative, he won his position on the committee. His win reminded me of Harmon's advice to "work on the inside" as a decision maker. As a member of the committee, Gullapalli sought out green political candidates to endorse on the local, state, and national levels. He also worked with current politicians to set and push through a green agenda.

"In the Sierra Club, anybody can be a leader, it just depends on the work you are ready to put in," says Gullapalli. The club's decentralized structure allows for local people to take charge of leading their own chapters with their own projects. While he was serving on the committee, there was a club volunteer in her early twenties that was interested in political endorsements. A mere two years after joining, she was elected to be the Advocacy Chair of the Angeles chapter. Like this volunteer, any passionate activist can be the one elected and decide how to impact his or her community. As Gullapalli emphasized, "We are in dire need of young blood that will carry the banner and the fight into the future."

The Various Levels of Environmental Advocacy

THE SIERRA CLUB'S SECRET TO SUCCESS

What makes the Sierra Club so successful?

A. Passion

The passion of every individual member, when combined, creates an unstoppable activist force. "Sierra Club is mostly run by volunteers, and the strength in numbers—no matter the age or experience—is what makes Sierra Club so successful." The Sierra Club is filled with activism because of the **commitment** of its members.

The national impact of the Sierra Club can be traced back as the aggregate impact of all the individual chapters' projects. Everything begins small. Like Gullapalli said, you "don't have to be Mother Teresa, you can do what you can with what you have." We all need to take a stand, especially now, when environmental protections are lacking. Most importantly, *"a long-term fight requires long-term commitment."* Be **consistent** in your advocacy. Show up and volunteer.

B. Collaboration

The second secret to success is collaborating to promote sustainability in individuals **and** institutions. Their website title boasts: "Sustainability is a Strategy for our Economic Future,"[6] demonstrating that the Sierra Club does not see economics and sustainability as mutually exclusive. Instead, to promote sustainability, they work with the companies responsible for harmful emissions. On their website, they incorporate various sustainability frameworks for businesses, including waste and energy reduction programs, charitable giving, community outreach, local economic support, and the transference of wealth through the supply chain. The Sierra Club emphasizes the message for business owners to work toward sustainability by adopting these programs, writing *"Don't waste your positive company brand!"*[7]

C. Creativity

The Sierra Club's smaller grassroots projects are also integral to its success. These projects effectively address the local problems through creative and place-specific solutions.

For example, the South Dakota chapter took action when the Clay County Planning Commission proposed major deregulation of confined animal feeding operations (CAFOs) in the county. The proposal would have removed all limits on the size of animal confinements and permitted for construction in Aquifer Protection Zones. The apparent goal, backed by the Governor's Office of Economic Development, was to lure out-of-state and out-of-country money to build industrial dairies that would be operated primarily by poorly paid immigrant workers. Furthermore, under the proposed changes, the untreated waste from 5,600 cows could be stored in an open lagoon above an aquifer zone. Ultimately, the proposed revision would throw out legal protection for all bodies of water except fisheries and navigable streams.

To address this, the Sierra Club chapter members analyzed the county's CAFO Ordinance and the proposed changes. They began a campaign through social media and local newspapers to educate local residents on the implications of the proposal. As a result, on the day of the hearing, the courthouse meeting room was packed by Sierra Club members and local residents who testified against the proposal. Continuing opposition in subsequent meetings forced commissioners to back away from complete deregulation. The Sierra Club chapter successfully fought against the imposition of big money that would exploit clean water, air, and health by sending letters, advocating, and attending meetings.

Furthermore, state legislator Frank Kloucek worked together with the local Sierra Club chapter to create the "Kloucek Challenge." The challenge was designed to make the new swine facility in South Dakota environmentally friendly and a model for mandating construction for all swine facilities in the state. With pressure from the Sierra Club, the new facility was successful by 2017. It was completely enclosed and located a mile away from the general public, as well as equipped with biofilters to remove harmful particulates from the air to prevent health issues, such as swine flu.

The South Dakota chapter demonstrates that a single passionate chapter of eco-winners can effectively fight against hazardous animal and agriculture practices. When volunteers work together, they exert a formidable force, even against powerful, vested interests.

This reminded me of my friend's argument that the campaign against plastic straws is stopping people from paying attention to the bigger problems. Although there are greater issues to focus on, what I have learned so far from my interviews and research is that all eco-winners first start with small, easy, individual-centered fixes, like not using straws. In other words, they first center on their individual impact and then move on to address bigger issues by collaborating with others.

That is the power of the Sierra Club. People banding together with a common purpose are strong enough to take on the big problems that matter. Through collaboration, a team of eco-winners can accomplish much more than just one individual, and even more so when working with businesses and governments.

HOW TO BECOME AN ADVOCATE
1. Find where you can volunteer: search up "[your location] volunteer work"
2. Get involved in a variety of work: beach cleanups, community gardens, planting trees
3. Consistently show up: i.e., set aside time every weekend
4. Keep your eyes open for more opportunities and remember your goal!

TAKEAWAYS
The point is ... do not settle. If you do nothing to make an impact, don't expect to see a change. Any progress made on your goals will result in more opportunities for improvement. All volunteering requires is some your time and motivation. So, go out with your friends and family and leave your mark, whether it's a tree you plant or a beach you clean. You will feel good when you *do* good.

Yes, it will require some self-discipline. Some weekends, I dislike getting up early for volunteer work, but then I remind myself of what I stand for: clean air, water, and land for everyone.

Remember that before tackling the world's entire problems, start with yourself—your consumption and lifestyle habits—and then address your community. If you have the privilege to influence your country's politics, take advantage of it, there is no limit to the impact you can make.

CHAPTER 13

THE POWER OF WORKING WITH, NOT AGAINST

"It's just economics 101: When it's free to pollute, you get more pollution. But when there's a price to pay, industry will have an incentive to find low-cost carbon solutions. For innovators who find safe and workable solutions to global warming, the rewards will be staggering."

—FRED KRUPP

After examining the decades-old Sierra Club, we now move onto another very powerful environmental interest group, the Environmental Defense Fund (EDF).

The EDF was originally started by a group of scientists that banded together to fight against the environmental consequences of the pesticide DDT. This original group of scientists lobbied the government and successfully got DDT banned state—and eventually nation—wide.[1] Since then, the Environmental Defense Fund has grown into one of the largest nonprofit environmental advocacy groups in the world. The EDF is known for its work on climate change, ecosystem restoration, oceans, and human health, and advocates using sound science, economics, and law to find environmental solutions that work.

INTRODUCING THE ENVIRONMENTAL DEFENSE FUND

The EDF consists of over seven hundred staff members and over two million members nationwide. Its headquarter office is located in New York City, with twelve other offices around the United States and a couple of international offices where scientists, researchers, and lobbyists work to promote environmental legislation.

Fred Krupp is the current president of the Environmental Defense Fund. He has guided the EDF for over three decades and throughout that time has focused on addressing the problem of methane emissions from the oil-and-gas system. He has also led EDF's innovative corporate partnerships with FedEx, McDonald's, and Walmart. Since he took his leadership position in 1984, EDF's annual operating budget has grown from $3 million to over $180 million, staff has increased from fifty to more than 700, and membership has expanded from 40,000 to over two million.[2]

Ever since I learned about the EDF, I have been fascinated with their work and curious as to how they grew to such proportion. To get some answers, naturally I took to messaging everyone associated with the EDF on LinkedIn.

When I got ahold of Fahad Huq, the recruiter for the EDF, I decided to interview him.

REPRESENTING THE EDF

Huq first became interested in environmental studies in high school. In his junior year, Global Kids, an organization that advocates for underprivileged communities, came to speak at his school. During the event, a guest-economist spoke about cap-and-trade and how it was an economic strategy to help the environment. Huq became fascinated with the topic and volunteered to help with the demonstration, after which he was offered an internship to help the economist in cap-and-trade research for his book. Although he was originally planning to follow his parents into a field of biology, he says that, "I understood that this is the bigger problem." The next year, Huq went to City of New York University (CUNY) where he majored in environmental science to study "the most complex, complicated system in the world," the Earth itself.

In college, Huq became involved in various environmental projects. At the time, CUNY was changing their infrastructure to become greener in response to the Bloomberg administration's "30 in 10" Challenge, a pledge to reduce greenhouse gas emissions by 30 percent within ten years.[5] This government challenge inspired the creation of the college's Sustainability Council and its ten-year Sustainability Plan. At first, the initiative was led by faculty and teachers, but it quickly expanded to the student council and other passionate students. Being part of student council and an environmental studies major, Huq got involved in the project and evaluated student proposals on how to reduce energy usage and make the campus greener. As a result of the students' initiative, different **creative** solutions were realized: the installation of bike racks and water filters, the planting of trees in urban spaces, the increase in recycling and compost bins, and their biggest project, the implementation of solar panels.

In 2011, solar panels were installed on the roof of the main campus to increase green energy use and encourage student participation in the field of renewable energy. Now, CUNY's Hunter College is cited as one of the "Greenest Colleges and Universities" and its sustainability achievements have been recognized by the Princeton Review, New York State Energy Research Development Authority, and more.[6]

After college, Huq ended up working as the recruiter for the Environmental Defense Fund, pursuing his passion for environmental advocacy.

THE SECRET OF THE ENVIRONMENTAL DEFENSE FUND
So, what makes the EDF so successful as an interest and advocacy group?

The secret is that EDF **works with corporations that harm the environment, instead of against them.**

"Corporate partnership is our biggest program," Huq explained. "The EDF is working with corporations to find a solution that will benefit both the company and the environment. *That* will be the future."

Increasing research studies are proving that financial incentives can be green. Companies are switching to sustainable supply chain models, and the success of EDF's environmental consulting demonstrates that. Only through effective partnerships does the EDF manage to have a broader influence.

A. McDonald's
Starting in 1986, the EDF first pushed McDonald's to implement biodegradable food-packaging containers.[7] Then, in 1990, they were the first group to partner with McDonald's to further improve packaging and reduce solid waste, which at the time was a groundbreaking corporate partnership. This partnership resulted from the protests of dozens of groups against the McDonald's restaurants' use of Styrofoam packaging in the 80s, and McDonald's way to save their public image.[8] Over twenty years later, the EDF continues to work with McDonald's to increase energy efficiency in restaurants all over the world.

B. Extractive Corporations
In 2000, seven of the world's largest extractive corporations partnered with the EDF to address climate change, setting firm targets to reduce their greenhouse gas emissions.[9] These natural resource companies include DuPont, Shell, Alcan Aluminium, BP Oil, Suncor Energy, Pechiney, and Ontario Power Generation. Philip E. Clapp, the president of the National Environmental Trust, states that these companies are being proactive and "making the appropriate management decision to start incorporating reductions into their

costs now rather than having to do them suddenly when there's a treaty in force and a law in place."[10] The EDF takes advantage of these companies' preemptive strategy with their environmental consulting sector.

C. Walmart

In 2005, the EDF partnered up with Walmart, another company notorious for their low sustainability index, and consulted Walmart on adopting new methods. The EDF helped Walmart reduce its greenhouse gas emissions from its manufacturing supply chain and prevent runoff by teaching its farmers how to efficiently use nitrogen-rich fertilizers. By the end of 2015, EDF helped Walmart reduce over twenty million metric tons of supply chain emissions—equivalent to taking off nearly six million cars off the road.[11] Today, with EDF's guidance, Walmart is committed to removing a gigaton of emissions—one billion tons—from its global supply chain by 2030. This reduction is equivalent to what Germany emits in a year, and comparable to taking 211 million cars off the road. The EDF writes, "It's an industry game-changer." And it really is, as more than 1,000 Walmart suppliers have already joined the effort, avoiding more than ninety-three million metric tons of greenhouse emissions in the last two years.[12]

D. US Political Sector

The EDF has also pushed through many important initiatives by working with the government. In 1990, the EDF designed Title IV of the Clean Air Act, incorporating market-based methods to cut air pollution and acid rain.[13] The new measures reduced sulfur dioxide pollution faster than expected, and at a fraction of the cost. From then on, the EDF continued to shape environmental policy. In 1995, they created their

"Safe Harbor" program, which led landowners of four million acres nationwide to welcome over sixty-three rare species to their land. In 2006, the EDF facilitated clean energy in California; and in 2012, they helped pass legislation that guaranteed funding for coastal restoration after the BP oil spill.[14]

TAKEAWAYS

The EDF is taking advantage of the new environmental norms and pushing them into businesses and governments. By working with the emitters, the EDF pioneered the idea that businesses and environmental organizations can mutually benefit from cooperation. Michael Bloomberg, founder of Bloomberg LP claims that "the EDF doesn't just talk about problems," but instead "helps design smart government policies, combines them with private sector know-how and creates solutions."[15] This creative solution is truly the EDF's eco-winner power move.

Huq himself affirmed, "Our core program has been copied so many times that now there are multiple chairs. The environmental consulting industry is growing quickly." The EDF has grown to become a reference point for all other environmental advocacy groups that are looking to make an impact in the private sector. Finishing the talk with Huq gave me hope. He told me, "Your generation specifically, is inventing a new brain. The generation before you is going to help, but you are the ones that are going to make and be affected by the changes. You will find that there are a lot of people like you out there."

CHAPTER 14

ECO-COMPANIES AND ECO-INDUSTRY

According to the 2017 report by the Carbon Disclosure Project, just one hundred companies are responsible for 71 percent of global carbon emissions, most of which produce coal, oil, and petroleum.[1]

Americans believe that the environment should be a priority for companies, according to the JUST Capital's 2015–19 survey.[2] However, corporate behavior is clearly not measuring up. The good news is that a number of companies across sectors are working to build a more sustainable future. Our job as eco-winners is to seek out these companies and support them while boycotting unsustainable goods.

In a 2019 study done by the *JUST Data Modeling & Environment* division, researchers tracked and analyzed the top environmental performers in thirty-five different industries.[3] These eco-companies not only had smaller impacts on the environment, but were also more equitable in their work force and wages. Environmental leadership also correlated with higher profitability, illustrated by the higher median Return-on-Equity earned by industry environmental leaders. This goes to show the mutually beneficial nature of an environmental agenda.

Now let's look at ten eco-companies across industries leading today's environmental movement.

ECO-COMPANIES

1. **Microsoft:** Software
   Since 2012, Microsoft's global operations have been 100 percent net carbon neutral, meaning that they charge a "carbon fee" to all business groups for their carbon footprint, and invest the fees collected into carbon reduction initiatives.[4]

2. **Intel:** Semiconductors and Equipment
   Intel believes in employee engagement to achieve their environmental goals. Since 2008, Intel has linked a portion of each employee's compensation to the achievement of their environmental sustainability metrics.[5]

3. **Ecosia:** Web Browser
   Ecosia is a tree-planting browser that uses the money earned from searches to fund reforestation programs and empower communities around the world. They have planted over eighty million trees in over 900 sites.[6] I personally really enjoy using Ecosia on my computer and phone!

4. **International Business Machines (IBM):** Computer Services
   In 2017, IBM purchased 22.9 percent of its electricity from renewable sources, exceeding its goal of 20 percent by 2020. The company is on track to reach 55 percent by 2025.[7]

5. **AT&T:** Telecommunications
   By 2020, AT&T aims to reduce all greenhouse gas emissions by 20 percent from its 2008 baseline—and as of 2017, the company had already reduced its emissions by 22.6 percent, surpassing its initial target.[8]

6. **General Motors:** Automobiles and Parts
   General Motors aspires to reduce its carbon footprint—of which 77 percent is represented by its global vehicle fleet—to zero. To achieve that goal, they plan to introduce twenty new zero-emissions vehicles to global markets by 2023.[9]

7. **General Mills:** Food, Beverage, and Tobacco
   General Mills tracks the sustainable sourcing of ten priority ingredients, including dairy milk and sugar beets, aiming to sustainably source 100 percent of these ingredients by 2020. By 2018, they had already achieved 85 percent.[10]

8. **Apple:** Technology Hardware
   In 2018, Apple sourced 100 percent of their facilities' electricity from renewable sources, and in 2017, twenty-two of Apple's supplier facilities were certified as "Zero Waste," including all iPhone final assembly sites.[11]

9. **JPMorgan Chase & Co:** Banks
   JPMorgan Chase aims to source 100 percent of its global power needs from renewable energy by 2020 and is committed to investing $200 billion in clean financing by 2025. It has already provided over $100 billion to the cause.[12]

10. **Kohl's Corp:** Retail
    Kohl's is committed to renewable energy use, and many of its stores derive up to 50 percent of their energy from solar power. The company has a total of 200,000 solar panels on 161 rooftops, as well as two wind turbines at one of its distribution centers.[13]

These companies show us that industries are changing. As environmental consciousness increases throughout the US and the world, businesses and legislation will change. Currently, many companies are starting to understand the financial incentive behind green methods. New companies such as Tesla, Bird, Ipsy, and Fjallräven are thriving because of environmental mission statements that their consumers want to support.

THE GROWING ENVIRONMENTAL INDUSTRY

The environmental sector is growing as well. Now, more than ever before, the professional sector is booming with environmental jobs. More banks are opening up branches in socially responsible investing (SRI), fueling investments in renewable energies and technologies, specifically green venture capital and cleantech.

Nearly $1 out of every $6 under professional management in the United States is a socially responsible investment, totaling $6.57 trillion.[15] Careers in environmental science are expected to increase by 11 percent, considerably faster than the average job according to the US Bureau of Labor Statistics.[16] The 2018 median salary for environmental specialists with bachelor degrees was $71,130.[17] Additionally, from 2013 to 2019, the number of environmental consulting businesses and their employees grew substantially. This increase in environmental science-related jobs is tied to the growing environmentally conscious habits of consumers and the subsequent rising number of environmental regulations set by governments.

Furthermore, industry is starting to understand the economic profitability of environmental policy. According to the Organisation for Economic Cooperation and Development, the cost of complying with environmental regulations amounts to roughly 2 percent of the GDP, whereas GDP has grown slightly less than 3 percent each year.[18] Thus, it can be concluded that the "burden" of environmental regulation is equal to the amount the economy grows each year. But even with this logic, this does not even account for the numerous environmental, public-health, social, and economic benefits of environmental regulations.[19]

The economy of our planet totals $75 trillion, but the positive externalities of ecosystem services (such as plants sequestering carbon dioxide, filtering air and water, and providing energy) are deemed free, not bearing any economic weight. At the same time, negative externalities such as waste and pollution are not being effectively regulated. Because of this, companies and governments are not being held accountable for irresponsible practices that harm the Earth.

The current economic standard represented by GDP is not an accurate measure of our global prosperity. Many are arguing for a switch-over to the Genuine Progress Indicator (GPI), one which takes pollution, resource depletion, education, and health into account. According to the GPI model, globally, our progress has flatlined for the last forty years, demonstrating that our current system of relying on extractive and environmentally harmful industries has been equally detrimental to the greater economy.

TAKEAWAYS

Industry and companies are changing. While many companies will resist the changing times, others are rapidly adjusting to the new sustainable model. Our job as eco-winners and consumers is to be conscious of the products and companies we support.

Unfortunately, an inconsistency between what consumers "want" and how they behave exists. For example, studies have shown that although 30–70 percent of consumers say they want to buy greener products, only 1–5 percent actually do.[20] If we all started consuming more sustainably, we could increase this percentage and inspire further environmental changes in industries.

CHAPTER 15

CORPORATIONS ≠ EVIL

"We cannot choose between growth and sustainability—we must have both."

—PAUL POLMAN, CEO OF UNILEVER

Companies continue to have tremendous influence on the planet and shape our carbon emissions and environments. After talking about changing industries in the last chapter, I wanted to discuss two corporate giants and how they have changed with the new environmental norms.

CORPORATION #1: AMAZON
Amazon is one of the biggest companies in the world, and chances are you bought something from them recently. However, Amazon has put massive pressure on the environment, especially with its fast shipping. Amazon currently releases about 44.4 million metric tons of CO_2 each year—equivalent to the total emissions of sixty-six power plants or ten million cars.[1]

With Amazon, two-day rush shipping is often "free" under Prime, but in reality, the environment is paying for it. To be shipped in two days, products across the country are transported by airplanes and aircrafts, which are **eight** times more energy intensive than trucks.[2] Not only that, but your package is oftentimes put into trucks that are not full just to meet the fast-shipping times, creating more unnecessary emissions. In the end, the carbon emissions for one- or two-day shipping can be as much as thirty-five times greater than for a fully loaded delivery van.[3] These inefficient routes are also more expensive, but they are "free" because Amazon is absorbing the delivery costs to fight for customers. Amazon creates a multitude of other environmental problems, including packaging waste, warehouse emissions, and worker conditions.

Still, Amazon is beginning to change. I first noticed this while visiting the Amazon Spheres in Seattle. The three spherical conservatories function both as employee workspaces and greenhouses, which house over 40,000 plants. Every floor of the Spheres represents a different rainforest habitat level with different temperatures and moisture concentrations to imitate the ecosystem of the plants on that level (e.g., the third floor represented a cloud forest with colder temperatures and more humidity).

I asked Sarah, one of the resident botanists, about the sustainability of the Spheres. According to her, the Spheres functioned as a breeding ground for threatened and endangered species that are currently being wiped out because of massive deforestation. The Spheres are devoted to sustainability: runoff water is constantly reused, specific lights with sensors turn off when light is coming from outside, and power is sourced from the excess heat of the neighboring Westin hotel. In addition, Amazon invests in green projects.

I was pretty surprised that Amazon had any sustainable initiatives at all. Considering Amazon is one of the largest companies in the world, I thought this was worth looking further into.

When I did my own research at home, I found that Amazon has a new worldwide Sustainability Department, which is currently launching the Amazon Sustainability Question Bank. The head of the department, Kara Hurst, affirmed that, "We believe in using our purchasing power to create more opportunities for renewables, which is why we're striving to power our global infrastructure using 100 percent renewable energy."[4]

Amazon has taken numerous steps toward becoming more environmentally friendly. In 2019, Amazon pledged to make 50 percent of all shipments carbon neutral by 2030 with their Shipment Zero program.[5] Amazon has also launched their largest wind farm in Texas, which contributes over one million megawatt hours of clean energy to the grid[6] and they are currently working to install fifty solar rooftops across their fulfillment center network by 2020.[7] These solar installations will potentially offset the CO_2 equivalent of more than 200 million miles of truck deliveries. The Solar Energy Industries Association ranked Amazon as number one in the United States for corporate solar installed in 2018.[8]

Amazon is also working to address packaging waste. Amazon introduced "frustration-free packaging" eleven years ago, the first of a suite of sustainable packaging initiatives that have eliminated 458,000 tons of packaging materials, avoiding over one billion shipping boxes.[9] Since then, they have teamed up with a range of different companies to create better products for the planet.

In 2018, Amazon partnered with Procter & Gamble to create the new Tide eco-Box that uses 60 percent less plastic and 30 percent less water than the comparable bottle. Brent Nelson, the Amazon engineer behind the transformation said, "This is a very important topic for our customers," and that the consumers "expect us to collaborate with selling partners to innovate and reduce packaging waste."[10] These small changes led by environmentally conscious individuals and the new eco-community help transform the type and quality of goods sold. With the growing awareness of climate change, waste, and the impacts we have on our planet, companies and brands like Amazon *want* to be more environmentally friendly, because they know that will ultimately help their business.

Amazon is also using their most powerful tool—purchasing power—to create more opportunities for renewables.[11] Amazon's investment in renewables is a powerful measure to help the environment, and its success will inspire other companies to act accordingly, leading to a greener economy. Hurst summarized this phenomenon with the quote: "I think the impact we're having is circular. We want to invest in renewables as a company, we want our associates to be proud to work in solar-powered buildings, and we want to be part of the new green economy and help create jobs in a high-growth industry."[12]

Lastly, Amazon is addressing the transportation problem I discussed in the beginning of the chapter. In July 2019, Amazon created a new shipping option called "Amazon Day" to help consolidate customers' deliveries into one drop-off per week. They also started offering discounts and rewards to shoppers who choose "no-rush shipping," which slows delivery times and decreases emissions.[13]

Even though Amazon still has a long way to go, its capacity for positive change demonstrates the power of consumers.

CORPORATION #2: UNILEVER
Unilever is a British-Dutch transnational consumer goods company that produces a variety of products.[14] Unilever is Europe's seventh most valuable company[15] with products sold to 2.5 billion consumers a day in 190 countries.[16] Unilever has around 400 brands including Dove, Axe, and Lipton.[17]

Unilever, like Amazon, is a profit-minded company with various unsustainable practices and products—in 2018 alone, Unilever emitted a total of sixty-one million tons of carbon dioxide. Since its establishment in 1929, Unilever has had a considerable impact on the planet.

However, also like Amazon, its company ethics and models have been changing. In 2010, Unilever created a Sustainable Living Plan that is central to their business model and aims to ensure that more of their products become sustainable.

This plan was set into motion by the new sustainably minded CEO Paul Polman, along with the rising environmental concern from consumers.

The Unilever **Sustainable Living Plan** has three big goals:

1. Helping more than one billion people improve their health and well-being
2. Halving the environmental footprint of Unilever products
3. Sourcing 100 percent of agricultural raw materials sustainably and enhancing the livelihood of people across the supply chain

Through the new Sustainable Plan, Unilever has committed itself to various ambitious environmental goals. In 2010, Unilever pledged to reduce the weight of their packaging by one-third and halve the waste associated with the disposal of their products. Unilever has already successfully decoupled the amount of packaging purchased. Since 2010, their total waste footprint per consumer has decreased by 31 percent.[18] Furthermore, in January 2017, Unilever pledged that 100 percent of their plastic packaging will be fully reusable, recyclable, or compostable by 2025.

Since the time their goals have been set, Unilever has developed completely recyclable products, reduced the size of packaging (including their Dove and TreSemme products), maximized the concentration of products for them to be diluted (saving 75 percent in plastic for the Brazil Omo laundry detergent), and sold refills to decrease the amount of packaging.

Unilever works with suppliers, nonprofits, governments, and other businesses to achieve their goals. The results of their efforts are evidenced by Unilever's 38 percent improvement in CO_2 efficiency from transport in kilogram per ton of products sold in 2018, as compared to their 2010 baseline.[19]

Furthermore, Unilever's Sustainable Living brands, brands that adhere to a higher set of sustainable standards, have delivered over 60 percent of the company's total growth, up 46 percent from the previous year.[20] The sustainable brands have grown 50 percent faster than the rest of their businesses, inspiring Unilever to adopt environmental models for more of their brands.

TAKEAWAYS

It is increasingly important to be part of a network, and we can do that by banding together as eco-winners. Unilever emphasizes "We know that the biggest challenges facing the world cannot be addressed by one company alone. So, we're also working to help transform the system in which business is done. By being part of the solution to challenges, businesses have the opportunity to win the trust of consumers while helping create societies and economies in which they can grow and succeed."[23]

Companies like Unilever and Amazon are powerful. Their decisions affect the environment around us significantly, and that is why I spent a chapter analyzing them and their new sustainability initiatives. Even though companies like Amazon and Unilever are profit-minded and advance environmental efforts for business purposes,[21] I think it is still important to see that companies have the potential to change. With this mindset, we will feel empowered to influence these industry giants.

The more I looked into the origins of Amazon and Unilever's sustainability, the more hope I had for the future of sustainability of other companies. As Amazon writes, "We are committed to and invested in sustainability because it's a win all around—it's good for business, the planet, our customers, and our communities."

CHAPTER 16

ECO-COUNTRIES CREATED BY ECO-WINNERS

―

"The change of energy supply is such a great task—it cannot be achieved by power supplies, by governments alone, you must have the citizens with you."

—URSULA SLADEK

Both states and industries have played a large role in causing climate change.[1] Specifically, industrialized countries including China, the United States, India, the European Union, Russia, and Japan are responsible for contributing the most emissions of various greenhouse gases (GHG).[2]

Specifically, the transportation industry is the largest single source of global GHG emissions and accounts for 29 percent of global emissions in 2017 with emissions coming from petroleum-based fuels burned for road, rail, air, and marine transportation. The electricity industry is the second largest source of GHGs, responsible for emitting 28 percent of global GHG emissions primarily through burning coal and natural gas for power. The agriculture and forestry industries are both responsible for about 20 percent of emissions from carbon and methane released from agriculture and livestock. Lastly, the chemical reactions in industry account for 22 percent of emissions and commercial and residential industries account for 12 percent of global emissions.[3]

However, the same wave of environmental consciousness pushed by eco-winners that is inspiring the shift in industry is also changing governments.

GERMANY'S MIRACLE COMMUNITY
In the small German village of Schonau lives eco-winner Ursula Sladek. In 1986, when Sladek was still a schoolteacher and mother of five, West Germany was powered by nuclear energy and coal. After the Chernobyl accident, Sladek was worried that radioactive residues from nuclear plants could negatively affect her community. Concerned about the safety of her community, Sladek and her husband sought to find a way to limit the amount of nuclear energy their community depended on.

Throughout her research, Sladek realized that energy companies were not letting citizens have any say in energy production decisions and nuclear energy, although considered green energy, had many safety issues. As a result, Sladek started

"Parents for a Nuclear Free Future" and initiated a campaign in the Black Forest region to encourage energy efficiency. The campaign gained traction and led the public to pay more attention to their energy consumption. With this newfound awareness and support, Sladek and her team set out to take on the local power grid operator and bring energy ownership back to the community. In 1997, she and her neighbors raised millions of euros that were needed to buy out the village's power grid and then turn it into an energy co-op. Sladek's project grew into the Schönau Power Supply (EWS), a co-op that is owned by about 1,000 people and provides power to more than 100,000 homes and businesses throughout the country.[5]

Since its establishment, EWS has created a more sustainable energy future for Germany. The company works like a non-profit that prioritizes its environmental and social benefits rather than its profits.[6] The majority of the company's profits are donated toward "investments for more renewable energy production facilities and outreach efforts that have helped several other towns in Germany set up their own community-owned energy companies."[7] EWS has grown annually, with total sales reaching sixty-seven million Euros in 2009.

Sladek continues to lead the company as president, continuing to inspire Germany to adopt sustainability ideals. Germany now strives to derive 100 percent of its power from renewable sources by 2050[8] and has implemented legislation designed to encourage individual and community efforts to increase renewable energies. In particular, Germany's Feed-In tariff obligates utilities to buy electricity from renewable installations, such as solar panels, at a price that guarantees a good return, this way encouraging companies to invest in renewable energies.⁹

The case of Ursula Sladek exemplifies how one eco-winner helped transform an entire country by committing to a goal, enrolling others in it, and pushing through a revolution. Sladek was **committed** and **consistent** in her mission to have her community not rely on nuclear energy, and she stuck with her project: first researching, then campaigning, and finally buying out the grid. Sladek was **creative** in her advocacy, transitioning to take on bigger goals after she saw how much support her initial campaign had garnered. Finally, Sladek was also **confident** in her mission, projecting her ideals onto the rest of Germany.

Sladek addressed climate change and energy security from the grassroots level, illustrating how social entrepreneurship and environmental stewardship can come together to tackle two of the world's most urgent challenges.

DENMARK'S RENEWABLES TRANSFORMATION
In 1980, Denmark introduced a 30 percent subsidy for investing in wind power. This pushed both small groups and larger communities to produce wind energy, and now energy cooperatives own about a fifth of Danish wind power with 175,000 households producing wind energy. These combined direct citizen and individual efforts transformed Denmark into a world leader in wind energy.¹⁰

Denmark's remarkable shift to renewable energy was started by eco-winners. In the 1970s, a group of young activists banded together to vocalize their antinuclear energy stance. They staged protests and wrote letters to elected officials, galvanizing a national antinuclear energy movement in the 1970s and 1980s until the Danish Parliament agreed to stop building nuclear reactors in 1985. But these eco-winners did not stop there. Instead, they then advocated for renewable alternatives and teamed up with similar-minded female politicians to "cooperate across parties to pass legislation supportive of renewable energy."[11]

1. **Commitment:** The activists were committed to fighting against nuclear reactors and waste, instead demanding renewable energy.
2. **Confidence:** With no action for ten years from the Parliament, protesters still had confidence that their efforts were not going unheard, demanding change.
3. **Consistency:** Protestors consistently fought, at first for an antinuclear energy movement and then for renewable energy solutions until Parliament responded.
4. **Creativity:** Protestors enrolled female politicians to help them enact new legislation that would make a renewable market in Denmark possible. Without this connection, the movement would not have become as impactful.

It is vital to use your individual power to make the change you want. The success of Denmark's transition toward renewable energy shows that by cooperating with like-minded people, you can catalyze a movement by enrolling others who can make an impact—such as the female politicians.

COSTA RICA'S REFORESTATION

Before World War II, almost 75 percent of Costa Rica was covered in forest. The next four decades devastated the country's forests. In just thirty-three years, from 1950 to 1983, more than 46 percent of forest land in Costa Rica was lost because of the lumber industry and the mass farming of coffee, sugar cane, and Africanized palm.[12] In the 1960s and 70s, Costa Rica had the highest per capita deforestation rate in the world.[13] The deforestation released large amounts of carbon into the atmosphere, devastated the rainforests, and threatened indigenous species including the poison dart frog. Starting in the 80s, it was evident that without government intervention, Costa Rica would suffer the same fate as Haiti and Nicaragua (which had devastated their ecosystems almost irreversibly).

The Costa Rican government stepped in and started enforcing various environmental measures including restricting logging permits, paying landowners that conserve their land, and attracting overseas investment in eco-tourism and pharmaceuticals. This created many jobs that depended on healthy rainforests and its ecosystem services. Hence, increasing attention was placed on preserving the forests and the deforestation rate gradually dropped to near zero.[14]

The trees began to grow back, and forests now cover almost half of the country, proving that the right policies can reverse environmental damage. Carlos Alvarado Quesada, the President of Costa Rica boasts that "We have managed not only to stop deforestation but to double forest coverage" as the economy grew. In fact, forests that covered 25 percent of the country in the 1980s covered more than 50 percent in 2013 according to the State of Nation report. Over that same time period, the country's GDP grew from $4 billion in 1983 to over $57 billion in 2013.

The readiness of key political figures to adopt out-of-the box creative and ethical decisions is mostly what realized these new realities to make Costa Rica greener and more prosperous.

The turning point came in 1948 when the government decided to disband their military.[15] Because of this decision, the country could then invest more of their funds into social and environmental programs. With the same mentality and value for ecosystems, Costa Rica amended its Constitution to honor the right of "every person ... to a healthy and ecologically balanced environment."[16]

Since 1997, nearly one million hectares of forest in Costa Rica have been part of the Payments for Ecosystem Services (PES) schemes that were implemented by the government. In these PES schemes, the people managing and using natural resources, typically forest owners or farmers, are paid to manage their resources to protect watersheds, conserve biodiversity, or capture carbon dioxide through tending or replanting.[17] However, not all projects realized themselves right away. The first forest laws restricting the amount of logging were at first unsuccessful and took about a decade for positive results and successful implementation to occur. It is only because of the new influx of ideas and the constant adaptation of these projects that there were such effective results.

A year ago, in February 2019, Costa Rica's President Carlos Alvarado Quesada launched an ambitious Zero-Carbon Plan, which is committed to ridding the country of fossil fuels by 2050.[18] Ninety-nine and a half percent of Costa Rica's electricity already comes from renewable energies, so the country's main area of work includes the fossil-fuel powered transportation sector. The government has enacted tax relief incentives for electric cars and other projects to replace buses with ones that can run on biofuels or other replacements.

In a speech, President Quesada expressed "Do you have at least five million people in the United States who want to do something about climate change? There! You already have more scale than Costa Rica. So, what is it [that] we provide—some inspiration perhaps, or some model or excuse."[19]

The point of this case study is not which of Costa Rica's strategies can be transferred to other countries, but that healthy economies are supported by healthy environments. This core idea has laid the foundations for decades of environmentally conscious decision-making within both the public and private sectors. This way, Costa Rica's greatest contribution to the world is its demonstration that "it is possible for a nation to establish a system of environmental ethics shared by the public and private sectors that carries benefits for the entire country."[19]

CALIFORNIA'S CAP-AND-TRADE

Cap-and-trade, or emissions trading, is a market-based approach to controlling pollution by providing economic incentives for achieving reductions in the emissions of pollutants. Principally, California set a cap across for carbon dioxide and related pollutants that drive global warming, allocated a limited number of permits to discharge carbon dioxide over a year, and decided the penalties for violations.

Throughout the years of implementation, the cap typically declines over time, providing "a growing incentive for industry and businesses to reduce their emissions more efficiently."[20] Hence, cap-and-trade works as companies that cut their pollution faster can sell allowances to companies that pollute more and because a limited amount of allowances are available, total pollution drops as the cap falls.

In 2013, California was the first state in North America to adopt a comprehensive carbon emissions trading program[21] during a time when national cap-and-trade was deemed too ambitious for the rest of the country. Because of the cap-and-trade program, California's emissions from sources subject to cap declined 8.8 percent between the programs' launch in 2013 and 2016; meanwhile, the economy has continued to thrive.[22]

The economic success of California's cap-and-trade inspired several other states—including the nine Northeast states of Connecticut, Delaware, Maine, Maryland, Massachusetts, New Hampshire, New York, Rhode Island, and Vermont—to establish their own carbon emissions programs.[23] Furthermore, California even inspired the international sphere in its market-based program. In 2017, China, the world's largest greenhouse gas emitter, took note from California and partnered with the Environmental Defense Fund to launch a national cap-and-trade program that covers more than

2,600 companies in regions with a population of more than 258 million.

TAKEAWAYS
The environmental policies of Schonau, Denmark, Costa Rica and California all demonstrate that setting an example can inspire others to take action. All of these cases also show that individual eco-winners are behind the changes of entire countries.

Eco-winners are revolutionary. They are the ones pushing through ideas and actions that were not pushed through before. They are the ones who are **courageously** and **confidently** leading their countries forward in the way they want countries to be led. They are the ones who take action when others sit around and wait. They have no doubt in their movements, enrolling others simply by doing what they are passionate about.

These case studies just go to show that there *is* hope for the world, hope that starts from the individual.

CONCLUSION

TIME TO STEP UP

"Study nature, love nature, stay close to nature. It will never fail you."

—FRANK LLOYD WRIGHT

While writing this book, I realized a couple of truths about myself.

1. I was not doing enough—and hypocritically, I was telling others to adopt a lifestyle that I did not fully adopt.
2. I was average in my efforts—not close to eco-winner material at all.

Realizing this put me in an awkward situation. If I truly wanted to make an impact (let alone inspire others), something had to change.

So, I came back to square one, my own footprint on the Earth.

I went online and took a Carbon footprint survey—I attached the link at the endnotes.[1] My footprint totaled 8.7 CO_2 emissions in ton per year and 4.8 gha of land to provide everything I consume—a concerning stat considering that our Earth has 1.7 gha available per person. The majority of my emissions, 1.5 global hectares (gha), were coming from transporation. My next biggest impacts were goods, at 1 gha, services, at another 0.9 gha. and shelter and food at 0.7 gha.

This compelled me to revisit my own advice.

REDUCE YOUR CARBON FOOTPRINT
1. Eat mindfully. Avoid meat and animal products. Source locally. Buy organic.
2. Advocate. Vote. Reach out to representatives in forms of letters, calls, and petitions. Attend committee meetings.
3. Volunteer. Join environmental organizations. Attend trail-work, clean-ups.
4. Be an ethical consumer. Be mindful of what you consume and from who.

To become more sustainable, I had to commit to lifestyle changes. To address transportation, I pledged to walk or take the bus to get around in Los Angeles. For goods, I reminded myself to not buy in excess by keeping a screenshot of my chart in Chapter 3. For services, I cooked for myself instead of eating out. I started to unplug my devices and grew a mini garden on my balcony with the help of my mom.

The point is, it is never too late to start. It is our time to make a difference. The world is changing and so are we. Passionate individuals from students and adults are a powerful force of change in the world. Now is the time to utilize this power. Take inspiration from eco-winners to leave your mark on the world.

"Individually, we are one drop. Together, we are an ocean."
—RYUNOSUKE SATORO

BIBLIOGRAPHY

CHAPTER 1

1 Damian Carrington. 2019. Greta Thunberg nominated for Nobel peace prize. *The Guardian*, sec. Environment. Available at <*https://www.theguardian.com/world/2019/mar/14/greta-thunberg-nominated-nobel-peace-prize*>. Accessed 16 January 2020.

2 Natalie Proulx. 2019. Learning With: "Becoming Greta: 'Invisible Girl' to Global Climate Activist, With Bumps Along the Way"—The New York Times. Available at <*https://www.nytimes.com/2019/02/21/learning/learning-with-becoming-greta-invisible-girl-to-global-climate-activist-with-bumps-along-the-way.html*>. Accessed 16 January 2020.

3 Greta Thunberg. 2019. Greta Thunberg (@gretathunberg) • Instagram photos and videos. Available at <*https://www.instagram.com/gretathunberg/*>. Accessed 17 January 2020.

4 Jonathan Watts. 2019. Greta Thunberg, schoolgirl climate change warrior: 'Some people can let things go. I can't.' *The Guardian*, sec. Environment. Available at <*https://www.theguardian.com/world/2019/mar/11/greta-thunberg-

schoolgirl-climate-change-warrior-some-people-can-let-things-go-i-cant>. Accessed 16 January 2020.

5 Mahita Gajanan. 2019. Greta Thunberg Gives Power Speech at UN Climate Summit | Time. *Time.* Available at <https://time.com/5684216/greta-thunberg-un-climate-action-summit-climate-speech/>. Accessed 27 January 2020.

6 Charlotte Alter, Suyin Haynes, and Justin Worland. n.d. Greta Thunberg Is TIME's 2019 Person of the Year. *Time.* Available at <https://time.com/person-of-the-year-2019-greta-thunberg/>. Accessed 27 January 2020.

7 Vaughan, Adam. n.d. Greta Thunberg: Why I began the climate protests that are going global. *New Scientist.* Available at <https://www.newscientist.com/article/mg24132213-400-greta-thunberg-why-i-began-the-climate-protests-that-are-going-global/>. Accessed 27 January 2020.

8 Greta Thunberg. 2019. Greta Thunberg (@gretathunberg) • Instagram photos and videos. Available at <https://www.instagram.com/gretathunberg/>. Accessed 17 January 2020.

9 NPR Staff. n.d. Transcript: Greta Thunberg's Speech At The U.N. Climate Action Summit. *NPR.org.* Available at <https://www.npr.org/2019/09/23/763452863/transcript-greta-thunbergs-speech-at-the-u-n-climate-action-summit>. Accessed 19 January 2020.

10 United Nations. 2019. *2019 Climate Action Summit Report.* Available at <https://www.un.org/en/climatechange/assets/pdf/CAS_closing_release.pdf>. Accessed 19 January 2020.

CHAPTER 2

1 Anthony Leiserowitz, Abel Gustafson, Edward Maibach, Seth Rosenthal, John Kotcher, Matthew Ballew, and Matthew Goldberg. 2018. *Climate Change in the American Mind: December 2018—Yale Program on Climate Change*

Communication. Available at <https://climatecommunication.yale.edu/publications/climate-change-in-the-american-mind-december-2018/2/>. Accessed 18 December 2019.

2 "The Tragedy of the High Seas." *The Economist*, Feb. 2014. *The Economist*, https://www.economist.com/leaders/2014/02/22/the-tragedy-of-the-high-seas.

3 Crutzen, Paul J. 2002. Geology of mankind. *Nature* 415 (6867): 23–23.

4 Bert Metz, Ogunlade Davidson, Heleen de Coninck, Manuela Loos, and Leo Meyer. 2005. *Carbon Dioxide Capture and Storage*. Available at <https://www.ipcc.ch/site/assets/uploads/2018/03/srccs_wholereport-1.pdf>. Accessed 19 January 2020.

5 Kim Ann Zimmermann, and 2017. n.d. Pleistocene Epoch: Facts About the Last Ice Age. *livescience.com*. Available at <https://www.livescience.com/40311-pleistocene-epoch.html>. Accessed 27 January 2020.

6 Crutzen, Paul J. 2002. Geology of mankind. *Nature* 415 (6867): 23–23.

7 GibbonsMar. 2, Ann, 2011, and 1:01 Pm. 2011. Are We in the Middle of a Sixth Mass Extinction? *Science | AAAS*. Available at <https://www.sciencemag.org/news/2011/03/are-we-middle-sixth-mass-extinction>. Accessed 27 January 2020.

8 National Research Council. 2011. *Climate Stabilization Targets: Emissions, Concentrations, and Impacts over Decades to Millennia*. Washington D.C. Available at <https://www.nap.edu/read/12877/chapter/8>. Accessed 19 January 2020.

9 Sterman, J. and L. Booth Sweeney (2007). Understanding Public Complacency About Climate Change: Adults' Mental Models of Climate Change Violate Conservation of Matter, *Climatic Change* 80(3-4): 213-238.

10 2020. Conservation Movement: Conservation Chronology 1912-1920. Available at <*http://lcweb2.loc.gov/ammem/ amrvhtml/cnchron6.html*>. Accessed 20 January 2020.

11 2020. New Deal. *Wikipedia*. Available at <*https://en.wikipedia. org/w/index.php?title=New_Deal&oldid=936260978*>. Accessed 20 January 2020.

12 Michael E. Kraft. n.d. *Environmental Policy and Politics (6th Edition): Michael E. Kraft: 9780205981809: Amazon. com: Books*. Available at <*https://www.amazon.com/ Environmental-Policy-Politics-Michael-Kraft/dp/0205981801*>. Accessed 18 December 2019.

13 Fernandez, Sonia. 2019. Climate undermined by lobbying: First-of-its-kind study quantifies the effects of political lobbying on likelihood of climate policy enactment. *ScienceDaily*. Available at <*https://www.sciencedaily.com/ releases/2019/05/190528193021.htm*>. Accessed 25 October 2019.

14 Josh Sager. 2018. Monsanto Controls Both the White House and the US Congress. *Global Research*. Available at <*https:// www.globalresearch.ca/monsanto-controls-both-the-white- house-and-the-us-congress/5336422*>. Accessed 19 January 2020.

15 Josh Sager. 2014. Monsanto's Revolving Door. *The Progressive Cynic*. Available at <*https://theprogressivecynic. com/2014/06/10/monsantos-revolving-door/*>. Accessed 19 January 2020.

CHAPTER 3

1 Robert Harris and A. V. Kneese, "Externalities: Economics and Thermodynamics, *Economy and Ecology: Towards Sustainable Development*."

2 Anne M Stark. 2017. Americans used more clean energy in 2016 | Lawrence Livermore National Laboratory. Available at <https://www.llnl.gov/news/americans-used-more-clean-energy-2016>. Accessed 26 December 2019.

3 American Council for an Energy-Efficient Economy. 2018. The International Energy Efficiency Scorecard. Text. *ACEEE*. Available at <https://aceee.org/portal/national-policy/international-scorecard>. Accessed 26 December 2019.

4 Jeff Harrison, "Study: Nation Wastes Nearly Half Its Food," *UA News,* November 18, 2004.

5 Frischmann, Chad. n.d. Opinion | The climate impact of the food in the back of your fridge. *Washington Post.* Available at <https://www.washingtonpost.com/news/theworldpost/wp/2018/07/31/food-waste/>. Accessed 20 January 2020.

6 Sierra Club. 2015. CAFO. *Sierra Club.* Available at <https://www.sierraclub.org/south-dakota/cafo>. Accessed 19 January 2020.

7 Mukhisa Kituyi, and Peter Thomson. 2018. Nearly 90% of fish stocks are in the red—fisheries subsidies must stop. *World Economic Forum.* Available at <https://www.weforum.org/agenda/2018/07/fish-stocks-are-used-up-fisheries-subsidies-must-stop/>. Accessed 20 January 2020.

8 Rosamond L. Naylor, Jason Clay, Rebecca J. Goldburg, Jurgenne Primavera, and Malcolm C. M. Beveridge. 2001. *Effects of Aquaculture on World Fish Supplies.* Washington D.C. Available at <https://www.esa.org/wp-content/uploads/2013/03/issue8.pdf>. Accessed 19 January 2020.

9 Doyle, Alister. "Ocean Fish Numbers Cut in Half Since 1970." *Scientific American,* Reuters, *www.scientificamerican.com/article/ocean-fish-numbers-cut-in-half-since-1970/.*

10 "How Much Water Does it Take to Make One Steak?" *PETA*, 2 Apr. 2015, *www.peta.org/videos/meat-wastes-water/*.

11 US Environmental Protection Agency, *Municipal Solid Waste in the United States 2009: Facts and Figures* (Washington DC colon EPA, 2010).

12 LeBlanc, Rick. n.d. How Long Will it Take That Bag of Trash to Decompose in a Landfill? *The Balance Small Business*. Available at <*https://www.thebalancesmb.com/how-long-does-it-take-garbage-to-decompose-2878033*>. Accessed 19 January 2020.

13 Princeton University. "A more potent greenhouse gas than carbon dioxide, methane emissions will leap as Earth warms." ScienceDaily. ScienceDaily, 27 March 2014. <*www.sciencedaily.com/releases/2014/03/140327111724.htm*>.

CHAPTER 4

1 "Veganism and the Environment." *PETA*, 6 Jan. 2019, *www.peta.org/issues/animals-used-for-food/animals-used-food-factsheets/vegetarianism-environment/*.

2 Environmental Working Group. 2011. Reducing Your Footprint—2011 Meat Eaters Guide | Meat Eater's Guide to Climate Change + Health | Environmental Working Group. Available at <*https://www.ewg.org/meateatersguide/a-meat-eaters-guide-to-climate-change-health-what-you-eat-matters/reducing-your-footprint/*>. Accessed 13 January 2020.

3 2014. Resources Spent on Consumption of Animals. *A new day dawning in Davis dining*. Available at <*https://coolcuisinedavis.wordpress.com/why-a-plant-based-diet/why-vegan-for-the-environment/resources-spent-on-consumption-of-animals/*>. Accessed 13 January 2020.

4 Martin Hickman. 2009. Study claims meat creates half of all greenhouse gases. *The Independent*. Available at <*http://*

www.independent.co.uk/environment/climate-change/study-claims-meat-creates-half-of-all-greenhouse-gases-1812909.html>. Accessed 13 January 2020.

5 Rhett A. Butler. 2020. Amazon Destruction. *Mongabay*. Available at <https://rainforests.mongabay.com/amazon/amazon_destruction.html>. Accessed 13 January 2020.

6 Earth Talks. 2009. Measuring the Daily Destruction of the World's Rainforests. *Scientific American*. Available at <https://www.scientificamerican.com/article/earth-talks-daily-destruction/>. Accessed 13 January 2020.

7 James Owen. 2005. Farming Claims Almost Half Earth's Land, New Maps Show. Available at <https://www.nationalgeographic.com/news/2005/12/agriculture-food-crops-land/>. Accessed 14 January 2020.

8 Croswell, Alexis. "Why Ag-Gag Laws Are a Threat to Us All." *One Green Planet*, One Green Planet, 13 Nov. 2015, www.onegreenplanet.org/animalsandnature/why-ag-gag-laws-are-a-threat-to-us-all/.

9 Wilson, Jerry. "Sustainability." *Sierra Club Fights for Sensible Regulation of Animal Feeding Operations*, South Dakota Sierra Club Chapter, 25 Nov. 2017, www.sierraclub.org/south-dakota/sustainability.

10 Shanker, Deena. 2015. Big Meat's wildly successful, 40-year crusade to keep its hold on the American diet. *Quartz*. Available at <https://qz.com/523255/the-us-meat-industrys-wildly-successful-40-year-crusade-to-keep-its-hold-on-the-american-diet/>. Accessed 20 January 2020.

11 Food and Agriculture Organization of the United Nations. n.d. Organic Agriculture: What are the environmental benefits of organic agriculture? *FAO*. Available at <http://www.fao.org/organicag/oa-faq/oa-faq6/en/>. Accessed 20 January 2020.

12 "New Evidence Confirms the Nutritional Superiority of Plant-Based Organic Foods," Organic Center, press release, March 18, 2008, *www.organic-center.org/news. pr.php?action=detail&pressrelease_id=22.*

13 Lyhn Johnson. n.d. National Geographic Freshwater 101: Food. *National Geographic.* Available at <*https://www.nationalgeographic.com/environment/freshwater/food/*>. Accessed 16 January 2020.

14 Frances Moore Lappé. 2011. *EcoMind.* Bold Type Books. Available at <*https://www.smallplanet.org/ecomind*>. Accessed 18 December 2019.

15 Renewable Energy Policy Network for the 21st Century, *Renewables 2010: Global Status Report* (Paris REN21 Secretariat, 2010).

16 Rachel Cleetus, Steven Clemmer, and David Friedman, *Climate 2030, A National Blueprint for a Clean Energy Economy* (Cambridge Massachusetts Union of concerned scientists) 2009 www.ucscu.org/global_warming/solutions/big_picture_solutions/climate-2030-blueprint. html.

17 National Council for Science and the Environment, David E. Blockstein, and Leo Wiegman, The Climate Solutions Consensus: What We Know and What to Do About It (Washington, DC: Island Press, 2010), 132.

18 REN21, *Renewables 2010*; Stephen Lovgren, "Costa Rica aims to be the First Carbon Neutral Country," National Geographic Daily News, March 7th, 2008.

19 Crystal Zheng. 2018. The Race to 100%: Renewable Energy-Powered Countries. Available at <*http://large.stanford.edu/courses/2018/ph240/zheng2/*>. Accessed 26 January 2020.

20 2015. Energy use in Sweden. *sweden.se*. Available at <*https://sweden.se/nature/energy-use-in-sweden/*>. Accessed 26 January 2020.

21 Robert Harris and A. V. Kneese, "Externalities: Economics and Thermodynamics, *Economy and Ecology: Towards Sustainable Development.*

22 Harvard University. 2013. Top 5 Steps to Reduce Your Energy Consumption. *Sustainability at Harvard*. Available at <*https://green.harvard.edu/tools-resources/poster/top-5-steps-reduce-your-energy-consumption*>. Accessed 26 January 2020.

23 U.S. Department of Energy. n.d. How Energy-Efficient Light Bulbs Compare with Traditional Incandescents. *Energy.gov*. Available at <*https://www.energy.gov/energysaver/save-electricity-and-fuel/lighting-choices-save-you-money/how-energy-efficient-light*>. Accessed 26 January 2020.

24 Environmental Protection Agency. 2014. Earth Month Tip: Power down | The EPA Blog. Available at <*https://blog.epa.gov/2014/04/07/earth-month-tips-power-down/*>. Accessed 26 January 2020.

25 Frances Moore Lappé. 2011. *EcoMind*. Bold Type Books. Available at <*https://www.smallplanet.org/ecomind*>. Accessed 18 December 2019.

CHAPTER 5

1 Anthony Leiserowitz, Abel Gustafson, Edward Maibach, Seth Rosenthal, John Kotcher, Matthew Ballew, and Matthew Goldberg. n.d. *Climate Change in the American Mind: December 2018—Yale Program on Climate Change Communication.* Available at <*https://climatecommunication.yale.edu/publications/climate-change-in-the-american-mind-december-2018/2/*>. Accessed 18 December 2019.

2 2019. Frances Moore Lappé. *Wikipedia*. Available at <https://en.wikipedia.org/w/index.php?title=Frances_Moore_Lapp%C3%A9&oldid=916826274>. Accessed 18 December 2019.

3 Frances Moore Lappé. 2011. *EcoMind*. Bold Type Books. Available at <https://www.smallplanet.org/ecomind>. Accessed 18 December 2019.

4 McKie, Bibi van der Zee Robin. 2009. Hundreds arrested at Copenhagen protest rally. *The Observer*, sec. Environment. Available at <https://www.theguardian.com/environment/2009/dec/12/hundreds-arrested-copenhagen-protest-rally>. Accessed 20 January 2020.

5 2020. Carbon offset. *Wikipedia*. Available at <https://en.wikipedia.org/w/index.php?title=Carbon_offset&oldid=936046842>. Accessed 20 January 2020.

6 Tipper, R. 2001. Fondo BioClimatico systems and procedures for the management of carbon services from rural communities and small scale farmers. *GOV.UK*. Available at <https://www.gov.uk/dfid-research-outputs/fondo-bioclimatico-systems-and-procedures-for-the-management-of-carbon-services-from-rural-communities-and-small-scale-farmers>. Accessed 29 October 2019.

7 Hewlett Foundation. n.d. Climate and Energy. *Hewlett Foundation*. Available at <https://hewlett.org/strategy/climate-and-energy/>. Accessed 20 January 2020.

8 Straughan, Baird, and Thomas H Pollak. n.d. *The Broader Movement: Nonprofit Environmental and Conservation Organizations, 1989-2005*. Washington D.C.: The Urban Institute.

9 O'Neill, Kate. 2017. *The Environment and International Relations*. Themes in International Relations. Cambridge: Cambridge University Press. Available at <https://www.

cambridge.org/core/books/environment-and-international-relations/B3A5682D44E0DA6FC4D3D5775B6CF9A8>.

CHAPTER 6

1 CNN, Isabelle Gerretsen. 2019. We are in the midst of an extinction crisis, warn UN scientists. *CNN*. Available at <*https://www.cnn.com/2019/05/06/world/one-million-species-threatened-extinction-humans-scn-intl/index.html*>. Accessed 21 January 2020.

2 Rebellion, Extinction. "About Us." *Extinction Rebellion*, 2018, rebellion.earth/the-truth/about-us/.

3 Alison Green; et al. (2018-10-26). *"Facts about our ecological crisis are incontrovertible. We must take action"*. The Guardian. Retrieved 2019-05-26.

4 *"Extinction Rebellion campaigners arrested in London"*. Green World. 2018-11-19. Retrieved 2018-11-24.

5 Matthew Taylor and Damien Gayle (2018-11-17). *"Thousands gather to block London bridges in climate rebellion"*. The Guardian. Retrieved 2019-05-26.

6 Rinvolucri, Bruno; Lamborn, Katie (2018-11-22). *"'We can't get arrested quick enough': life inside Extinction Rebellion—video"*. The Guardian. Retrieved 2019-05-26.

7 Sulda, Dixie (2019-04-15). *"Climate change protesters forcibly removed from Parliament House"*. The Advertiser. Adelaide. Retrieved 2019-05-26.

8 Watts, Jonathan (2018-12-10). *"Extinction Rebellion goes global in run-up to week of international civil disobedience"*. The Guardian. Retrieved 2018-05-26.

9 *"Extinction Rebellion"*. Brightest. 2019-01-13. Retrieved 2019-05-26.

10 April 23, Posted on, and 2019. 2019. Extinction Rebellion: A new stage for the climate change movement. Available at <https://climateandcapitalism.com/2019/04/23/xr-protests-a-watershed-for-the-climate-change-movement/, https://climateandcapitalism.com/2019/04/23/xr-protests-a-watershed-for-the-climate-change-movement/>. Accessed 26 January 2020.

11 Taylor, Matthew. "The Extinction Rebellion Scorecard: What Did It Achieve?" *The Guardian*, Guardian News and Media, 25 Apr. 2019, *www.theguardian.com/environment/2019/apr/25/extinction-rebellion-assessing-the-impact*.

12 Ibid.

13 Gabbatis, John, and Simon Evans. "In-Depth: The UK Should Reach 'Net-Zero' Climate Goal by 2050, Says CCC." *Carbon Brief*, 3 May 2019, *www.carbonbrief.org/in-depth-the-uk-should-reach-net-zero-climate-goal-by-2050-says-ccc*.

14 Taylor, Matthew. "The Extinction Rebellion Scorecard: What Did it Achieve?" *The Guardian*, Guardian News and Media, 25 Apr. 2019, *www.theguardian.com/environment/2019/apr/25/extinction-rebellion-assessing-the-impact*.

CHAPTER 7

1 Lisa Merton, and Alan Dater. 2008. *Taking Root Documentary*. The Green Belt movement. Available at <https://www.greenbeltmovement.org/wangari-maathai/taking-root-documentary>. Accessed 19 December 2019.

2 Ibid.

3 Missouri Botanical Garden. 2002. Why Are Wetlands Important? Available at <http://www.mbgnet.net/fresh/wetlands/why.htm>. Accessed 19 December 2019.

4 Program, NOAAs Coral Reef Conservation. "NOAA's Coral Reef Conservation Program (CRCP)." *NOAA Coral Reef Conservation Program (CRCP)*, National Oceanic and Atmospheric Administration, 12 Oct. 2007, coralreef.noaa.gov/.

5 N.d. East Africa Living Encyclopedia. University of Pennsylvania. Available at <https://www.africa.upenn.edu/NEH/khistory.htm>. Accessed 22 January 2020.

6 Lisa Merton, and Alan Dater. 2008. *Taking Root Documentary.* The Green Belt movement. Available at <https://www.greenbeltmovement.org/wangari-maathai/taking-root-documentary>. Accessed 19 December 2019.

7 The Green Belt movement. n.d. The Green Belt movement. Available at <http://www.greenbeltmovement.org/>. Accessed 20 December 2019.

8 Nanjala Nyabola. 2015. Wangari Maathai was not a good woman. Kenya needs more of them. *African Arguments*. Available at <https://africanarguments.org/2015/10/06/wangari-maathai-was-not-a-good-woman-kenya-needs-many-more-of-them/>. Accessed 22 January 2020.

9 Kirwa, Alex. 2019. The Only Woman Who Gave Moi Sleepless Nights. *Daily Active*. Available at <https://www.dailyactive.info/2019/10/10/the-only-woman-who-gave-moi-sleepless-nights/>. Accessed 22 January 2020.

10 N.d. Oct. 8, 2004: Wangari Maathai Awarded the Nobel Peace Prize. *Zinn Education Project*. Available at <https://www.zinnedproject.org/news/tdih/wangari-maathai/>. Accessed 22 January 2020.

11 Geocaching. n.d. Geocaching—The Official Global GPS Cache Hunt Site. Available at <http://www.geocaching.com/>. Accessed 25 February 2020.

CHAPTER 8

1 Karl Mathiesen. 2015. May Boeve: the new face of the climate change movement | Environment | The Guardian. Available at <https://www.theguardian.com/environment/2015/apr/08/may-boeve-new-face-of-climate-change-movement-350-org>. Accessed 20 December 2019.

2 US Department of Commerce, NOAA. 2019. ESRL Global Monitoring Division—Global Greenhouse Gas Reference Network. Available at <https://www.esrl.noaa.gov/gmd/ccgg/trends/>. Accessed 20 December 2019.

3 350.org. 2009. A global campaign to confront the climate crisis. *350.org*. Available at <https://350.org/>. Accessed 23 January 2020.

4 350.org. n.d. Divestment and the History of 350.org. *350.org*. Available at <https://350.org>. Accessed 20 December 2019.

5 Grist, From, and part of the Guardian Environment Network. 2009. Groups use 350's big day to fight cap-and-trade. *The Guardian*, sec. Environment. Available at <https://www.theguardian.com/environment/2009/oct/23/network-climate-change>. Accessed 20 December 2019.

6 2009. In pictures: The 350.org climate change worldwide protest. *The Guardian*, sec. Environment. Available at <https://www.theguardian.com/environment/gallery/2009/oct/27/350-campaign-climate-change-protest>. Accessed 20 December 2019.

7 The Associated Press, and 2019 11:01 AM MT | Last Updated: March 25. n.d. Pipeline giant Enbridge spends $11M US lobbying Minnesota leaders | CBC News. *CBC*. Available at <https://www.cbc.ca/news/canada/calgary/enbridge-energy-lobbying-minnesota-pipeline-1.5069529>. Accessed 20 December 2019.

8 Elizabeth E. Payne. 2017. Who Profits from the Pipelines? > Appalachian Voices. *Appalachian Voices*. Available at <*http://appvoices.org/2017/04/13/who-profits-from-the-pipelines/*>. Accessed 20 December 2019.

9 Ibid.

10 Amy Goodman. 2018. *Interview with Winona LaDuke*. Available at <*http://archive.org/details/dn2018-1207_vid*>. Accessed 20 December 2019.

11 Miranda Green. 2018. Ocasio-Cortez joins climate change sit-in at Pelosi's office | TheHill. Available at <*https://thehill.com/policy/energy-environment/416411-youth-protestors-fill-nancy-pelosis-office-demanding-climate-change*>. Accessed 23 January 2020.

12 Nina Sheridan. 2018. May Boeve: How Sonomans can get involved in climate change action. Sonoma Index Tribune. Available at <https://www.sonomanews.com/news/7987493-181/may-boeve-how-sonomans-can>. Accessed 25 February 2020.

CHAPTER 9

1. The Hidden Costs of Industrial Agriculture. *Union of Concerned Scientists* https://www.ucsusa.org/resources/hidden-costs-industrial-agriculture.

2. Prabhu L. Pingali. Green Revolution: Impacts, limits, and the path ahead. *Proc. Natl. Acad. Sci.* 109, 12302–12308 (2012).

3. Aktar, Md. W., Sengupta, D. & Chowdhury, A. Impact of pesticides use in agriculture: their benefits and hazards. *Interdiscip. Toxicol.* 2, 1–12 (2009).

4. Amadeo, K. How Farm Subsidies Affect You. *The Balance* https://www.thebalance.com/farm-subsidies-4173885.

5. U.S. Department of Agriculture. 2012 Census Highlights: Farm Economics. *http://farm.ewg.org/*.

6. Craig Cox & Anne Weir Schechinger. Federal Crop Insurance Policy Could Lead to Second 'Dust Bowl'. *EWG https://www.ewg.org/research/federal-crop-insurance-policy-leading-another-dust-bowl*.

7. Joseph W. Glauber, Barry K. Goodwin, Vincent H. Smith & Daniel A. Sumner. *Agricultural policy in disarray: Reforming the farm bill—an overview. https://www.aei.org/research-products/report/agricultural-policy-in-disarray-reforming-the-farm-bill-an-overview/*.

8. Reforming Federal Farm Policies. *Cato Institute https://www.cato.org/publications/tax-budget-bulletin/reforming-federal-farm-policies* (2018).

9. Edwards, C. Agricultural Subsidies. *Downsizing the Federal Government https://www.downsizinggovernment.org/agriculture/subsidies* (2018).

10. Josh Sewell, "Subsidies to Address Risk Are Harmful," in "Farms and Free Enterprise: A Blueprint for Agricultural Policy," ed. Daren Bakst, Heritage Foundation, 2016.

11. Claydon, S. Health Effects of Pesticides. *Pesticide Action Network UK https://www.pan-uk.org/health-effects-of-pesticides/*.

12. Farm Case Study: Soul Fire Farm. *Stone Barns Center https://www.stonebarnscenter.org/resource/farm-case-study-soul-fire-farm/*.

13 Katie Pace. 2015. Indigenous Agriculture and Sustainable Food. Available at <*https://sustainablefoodcenter.org/latest/gardening/indigenous-agriculture-and-sustainable-food*>. Accessed 24 January 2020.

14 Wilson, Gilbert (1917). Agriculture of the Hidatsa Indians: An Indian Interpretation. Gloucestershire: Dodo Press. p. 25. ISBN 978-1409942337.

15 SOUL FIRE FARM. *SOUL FIRE FARM http://www. soulfirefarm.org/.*

16 David Howard King. 2018. Soul Fire Farm is giving the land, and its bounty, back to the people. The Collaborative. Available at <http://collaborativemagazine.org/2018/11/19/5860/>. Accessed 25 February 2020.

CHAPTER 10

1 TEDx Talk. n.d. *How to Turn Advocacy Into Action | Heidi Harmon | TEDxSanLuisObispo.* Available at *<https://www.youtube.com/watch?v=CH8OPz4WKE0>.* Accessed 21 December 2019.

2 Heidi Harmon. 2014. Full Biography for Heidi Harmon. Smart Voters. Available at <http://www.smartvoter.org/2014/11/04/ca/state/vote/harmon_h/bio.html>. Accessed 25 February 2020.

3 TEDx Talk. n.d. *How to Turn Advocacy Into Action | Heidi Harmon | TEDxSanLuisObispo.* Available at *<https://www.youtube.com/watch?v=CH8OPz4WKE0>.* Accessed 21 December 2019.

4 Nick Wilson. 2018. SLO wants to be carbon-neutral 10 years faster than the rest of California. *sanluisobispo.* Available at *<https://www.sanluisobispo.com/news/local/environment/article218938825.html>.* Accessed 22 December 2019.

5 Pratt, Tyler. n.d. San Luis Obispo works to improve bicycle safety. Available at *<https://www.kcbx.org/post/san-luis-obispo-works-improve-bicycle-safety>.* Accessed 23 January 2020.

6 Nick Wilson. 2019. SLO council passes policy to make new buildings all-electric—but gas is still an option. *sanluisobispo*. Available at <https://www.sanluisobispo.com/news/local/environment/article234680472.html>. Accessed 22 December 2019.

7 Leon Koenen. 2011. San Luis Obispo: The First City with a Major Public Smoking Ban | KCET. Available at <https://www.kcet.org/socal-focus/san-luis-obispo-the-first-city-with-a-major-public-smoking-ban>. Accessed 22 December 2019.

8 Ladin, Ashley, and Kylie Kowalske. 2018. "Meet Mayoral Candidate Heidi Harmon." Mustang News, October 30, 2018. *https://mustangnews.net/meet-mayoral-candidate-heidi-harmon/*.

9 "CIRCLE » Young People Dramatically Increase Their Turnout to 31%, Shape 2018 Midterm Elections." *CIRCLE RSS, civicyouth.org/young-people-dramatically-increase-their-turnout-31-percent-shape-2018-midterm-elections/*.

10 Center for Information and Research on Civic Learning and Engagement. 2018. CIRCLE » From #Parkland to the Polls: Teen Activism and Youth Voting in 2018. Available at <https://civicyouth.org/from-parkland-to-the-polls-teen-activism-and-youth-voting-in-2018/>. Accessed 22 December 2019.

11 Michael P. McDonald. 2018. *early_2018—United States Elections Project*. Available at <http://www.electproject.org/early_2018>. Accessed 22 December 2019.

12 CIRCLE » Young People Dramatically Increase Their Turnout to 31%, Shape 2018 Midterm Elections." *CIRCLE RSS, civicyouth.org/young-people-dramatically-increase-their-turnout-31-percent-shape-2018-midterm-elections/*.

CHAPTER 11

1 N.d. *"Guest Post: Dierdre Wolownick "Life of Learning"*. Picky Bars.

2 Duane, Daniel (March 12, 2015). *"The Heart-Stopping Climbs of Alex Honnold"*. The New York Times Magazine. Retrieved October 14, 2018. Honnold could afford to buy a decent home, if that interested him. But living in a van—a custom-outfitted van, in his case, with a kitchenette and cabinets full of energy bars and climbing equipment—represents freedom.

3 Weidner, Chris. "Chris Weidner: The Outrageous Simplicity of Alex Honnold, the World's Boldest Climber." *Boulder Daily Camera*, 13 June 2017, www.dailycamera.com/2017/06/13/chris-weidner-the-outrageous-simplicity-of-alex-honnold-the-worlds-boldest-climber/.

4 *"To Be the Best Rock Climber Is to Earn As Much As an Orthodontist"*. Wealthsimple Magazine. March 20, 2018. Retrieved February 19, 2019.

5 *Alex Honnold's Van Life. Outside Online* (video). July 28, 2014. Retrieved February 26, 2019.

6 Lowther, Alex (Summer 2011). *"Less and Less Alone: Alex Honnold"*. Alpinist. Retrieved October 14, 2018.

7 McCarthy, Tom (June 4, 2017). *"Rock climber makes historic ropeless ascent of California's El Capitan"*. The Guardian. Retrieved June 5, 2017.

8 Brad Rassler. n.d. The Greening of Alex Honnold. *Sustainable Play*. Available at <https://sustainableplay.com/the-greening-of-alex-honnold/>. Accessed 26 January 2020.

9 Honnold Foundation. n.d. Honnold Foundation. *Honnold Foundation*. Available at <http://www.honnoldfoundation.org>. Accessed 26 January 2020.

10 Environmental Protection Agency. 2016. *GRID Alternatives: Solar Programs in Underserved Communities*. Available at <https://www.epa.gov/sites/production/files/2017-06/documents/grid_alternatives_profile_508.pdf>. Accessed 27 January 2020.

11 GRID Alternatives. n.d. GRID Alternatives | People. Planet. Employment. Available at <https://gridalternatives.org/>. Accessed 26 January 2020.

12 2020. Casa Pueblo • Puerto Rico—Organización de Autogestión Comunitaria. *Casa Pueblo*. Available at <http://casapueblo.org/>. Accessed 26 January 2020.

13 N.d. North End Woodward Community Coalition. *Honnold Foundation*. Available at <http://www.honnoldfoundation.org/newccpartner>. Accessed 27 January 2020.

14 2016. Building the Engine. Available at <buildingtheengine.com>. Accessed 27 January 2020.

15 N.d. Solar Energy Foundation. *Honnold Foundation*. Available at <http://www.honnoldfoundation.org/sef>. Accessed 27 January 2020.

16 N.d. The Solar Foundation—Advancing Solar Energy Use—Nonprofit. *The Solar Foundation*. Available at <https://www.thesolarfoundation.org/>. Accessed 27 January 2020.

17 Brad Rassler. n.d. The Greening of Alex Honnold. *Sustainable Play*. Available at <https://sustainableplay.com/the-greening-of-alex-honnold/>. Accessed 26 January 2020.

18 N.d. Honnold Foundation. *Honnold Foundation*. Available at <http://www.honnoldfoundation.org>. Accessed 27 January 2020.

CHAPTER 12

1 Sierra Club. n.d. About the Sierra Club. Available at <https://www.sierraclub.org/about-sierra-club>. Accessed 22 December 2019.

2 Sierra Club. n.d. About—The John Muir Exhibit—Sierra Club. Available at <https://vault.sierraclub.org/john_muir_exhibit/about/>. Accessed 22 December 2019.

3 Kloucek, Frank. "Sustainability." *The Kloucek Challenge (Editorial)*, South Dakota Sierra Club Chapter, 25 Nov. 2017, www.sierraclub.org/south-dakota/sustainability.

4 Croswell, Alexis. "Why Ag-Gag Laws Are a Threat to Us All." *One Green Planet*, One Green Planet, 13 Nov. 2015, www.onegreenplanet.org/animalsandnature/why-ag-gag-laws-are-a-threat-to-us-all/.

5 Wilson, Jerry. "Sustainability." *Sierra Club Fights for Sensible Regulation of Animal Feeding Operations*, South Dakota Sierra Club Chapter, 25 Nov. 2017, www.sierraclub.org/south-dakota/sustainability.

6 Sierra Club South Dakota. 2015. Sustainability. *Sierra Club*. Available at <https://www.sierraclub.org/south-dakota/sustainability>. Accessed 23 December 2019.

7 Ibid.

8 Ibid.

CHAPTER 13

1 US EPA, OA. n.d. DDT Regulatory History: A Brief Survey (to 1975). Reports and Assessments. Available at <ddt-regulatory-history-brief-survey-1975.html>. Accessed 25 January 2020.

2 Environmental Defense Fund. n.d. Fred Krupp. *Environmental Defense Fund*. Available at <https://www.edf.org/people/fred-krupp>. Accessed 26 December 2019.

3 Bureau of Labor Statistics, U.S. Department of Labor, Occupational Outlook Handbook, Environmental Scientists and Specialists, on the Internet at https://www.bls.gov/ooh/life-physical-and-social-science/environmental-scientists-and-specialists.htm.

4 Ibis World. 2019. *IBISWorld—Industry Market Research, Reports, and Statistics*. Available at <https://www.ibisworld.com/default.aspx>. Accessed 26 December 2019.

5 Hunter College Sustainability Council. n.d. The Hunter College Sustainability Council (HCSC)—Hunter College. Available at <http://www.hunter.cuny.edu/huntergreen/about/the-hunter-college-sustainability-council-hcsc>. Accessed 26 December 2019.

6 Hunter College Sustainability Council. n.d. SUSTAINABLE EDUCATION & OUTREACH—Hunter College. Available at <http://www.hunter.cuny.edu/huntergreen/copy_of_green-initiatives/sustainable-education-outreach>. Accessed 26 December 2019.

7 "The Nation: Environmentalists Try to Move the Markets," by John Holusha, The New York Times, August 22, 1993.

8 Holusha, John. 1990. Packaging and Public Image: McDonald's Fills a Big Order. *The New York Times*, sec. Business. Available at <https://www.nytimes.com/1990/11/02/business/packaging-and-public-image-mcdonald-s-fills-a-big-order.html>. Accessed 25 January 2020.

9 Revkin, Andrew C. 2000. 7 Companies Agree to Cut Gas Emissions. *The New York Times*, sec. Business. Available at <https://www.nytimes.com/2000/10/18/business/7-companies-agree-to-cut-gas-emissions.html>. Accessed 25 January 2020.

10 Ibid.

11 Environmental Defense Fund. n.d. Our partnership with Walmart brings big change. *Environmental Defense Fund*. Available at <*https://www.edf.org/partnerships/walmart*>. Accessed 25 January 2020.

12 Ibid.

13 Shabecoff, Philip, and Special To the New York Times. 1985. Consensus Is Seen to Curb Acid Rain. *The New York Times*, sec. U.S. Available at <*https://www.nytimes.com/1985/10/18/us/consensus-is-seen-to-curb-acid-rain.html*>. Accessed 25 January 2020.

14 Environmental Defense Fund. 2019. Key achievements from our past. *Environmental Defense Fund*. Available at <*https://www.edf.org/success-stories/past*>. Accessed 27 December 2019.

15 Environmental Defense Fund. n.d. How we get results. *Environmental Defense Fund*. Available at <*https://www.edf.org/how-we-get-results*>. Accessed 27 December 2019.

CHAPTER 14

1 Riley, Tess. 2017. Just 100 companies responsible for 71% of global emissions, study says. The Guardian, sec. Guardian Sustainable Business. Available at <*https://www.theguardian.com/sustainable-business/2017/jul/10/100-fossil-fuel-companies-investors-responsible-71-global-emissions-cdp-study-climate-change*>. Accessed 25 December 2019.

2 "Polling the American People." 2015. JUST Capital (blog). 2019 2015. *https://justcapital.com/polling/*.

3 Yusuf George. n.d. The Top 33 Companies For The Environment By Industry. Forbes. Available at <*https://www.forbes.com/sites/justcapital/2019/04/22/the-top-33-companies-*

for-the-environment-by-industry/>. Accessed 27 December 2019.

4 Microsoft. n.d. Environmental Sustainability—Microsoft CSR. Available at <https://www.microsoft.com/en-us/corporate-responsibility/sustainability>. Accessed 27 December 2019.

5 Intel. n.d. Intel and the Environment. Intel. Available at <https://www.intel.com/content/www/us/en/environment/intel-and-the-environment.html>. Accessed 27 December 2019.

6 Ecosia. 2019. Ecosia is the search engine that plants trees. Available at <https://info.ecosia.org/what?ref=fb-share>. Accessed 27 December 2019.

7 IBM. 2019. IBM and the Environment—Climate protection—Renewable electricity consumption. CTB30. Available at <www.ibm.com/ibm/environment/climate/renewable_energy.shtml>. Accessed 27 December 2019.

8 AT&T. 2017. AT&T Corporate Responsibility Update: Building a Better Tomorrow. Available at <https://about.att.com/ecms/dam/csr/sustainability-reporting/PDF/2018/ATT-Corporate-Responsibility-Update.pdf>. Accessed 27 December 2019.

9 General Motors. 2017. General Motors 2017 Sustainability Report. Available at <https://www.gmsustainability.com/_pdf/downloads/GM_2017_SR.pdf>.

10 General Mills. 2019. General Mills: Sustainable sourcing. Available at <http://www.generalmills.com/en/Responsibility/Sustainability/sustainable-sourcing>. Accessed 27 December 2019.

11 Apple. n.d. Environment. Apple (Latin America). Available at <https://www.apple.com/lae/environment/>. Accessed 27 December 2019.

12 IPM. 2018. IBM and the Environment—Climate protection—Renewable electricity consumption. Available at <https://www.ibm.com/ibm/environment/climate/renewable_energy.shtml>. Accessed 27 December 2019.

13 Kohl's. 2018. CSR Report Highlights Family Health & Wellness. Kohls Corporation. Available at <http://corporate.kohls.com/news/archive-/2019/April/csr-report-highlights-family-health---wellness>. Accessed 27 December 2019.

14 Bureau of Labor Statistics, U.S. Department of Labor, Occupational Outlook Handbook, Environmental Scientists and Specialists, on the Internet at https://www.bls.gov/ooh/life-physical-and-social-science/environmental-scientists-and-specialists.htm.

15 The Forum for Sustainable and Responsible Investment. 2018. 2018 edition of the US SIF Foundation's Report on US Sustainable, Responsible and Impact Investing Trends. Available at <https://www.ussif.org/trends>. Accessed 25 January 2020.

16 Ibis World. 2019. IBISWorld—Industry Market Research, Reports, and Statistics. Available at <https://www.ibisworld.com/default.aspx>. Accessed 27 December 2019.

17 2019. Venture philanthropy. Wikipedia. Available at <https://en.wikipedia.org/w/index.php?title=Venture_philanthropy&oldid=931827115>. Accessed 28 December 2019.

18 1990. Economics and the Environment: A Survey of Issues and Policy Options. OECD Economics Department Working Papers. Available at <https://www.oecd-ilibrary.org/economics/economics-and-the-environment_658785422370>. Accessed 25 January 2020.

19 Michael E. Kraft. n.d. Environmental Policy and Politics (6th Edition): Michael E. Kraft: 9780205981809: Amazon.com: Books. Available at <https://www.amazon.com/

Environmental-Policy-Politics-Michael-Kraft/dp/0205981801>. Accessed 18 December 2019.

20 O'Rourke, Dara, and Abraham Ringer. 2015. The Impact of Sustainability Information on Consumer Decision Making. Journal of Industrial Ecology 20.

CHAPTER 15

1 2019. Carbon footprint. *Sustainability—US*. Available at <https://sustainability.aboutamazon.com/carbon-footprint>. Accessed 25 January 2020.

2 Lydia DePillis. 2019. America's addiction to absurdly fast shipping has a hidden cost. *CNN*. Available at <https://www.cnn.com/2019/07/15/business/fast-shipping-environmental-impact/index.html>. Accessed 2 January 2020.

3 John General, and Richa Naik. 2019. *America's addiction to absurdly fast shipping has a hidden cost.* CNN Business. Available at <https://www.cnn.com/2019/07/15/business/fast-shipping-environmental-impact/index.html>. Accessed 2 January 2020.

4 Tom Murray. 2018. Amazon's Big Opportunity: Transparency In Sustainability. *Forbes*. Available at <https://www.forbes.com/sites/edfenergyexchange/2018/04/02/amazons-big-opportunity-transparency-in-sustainability/#5cf239967c50>. Accessed 2 January 2020.

5 Amazon. 2019. Delivering Shipment Zero, a vision for net zero carbon shipments. *US Day One Blog*. Available at <https://blog.aboutamazon.com/sustainability/what-is-shipment-zero>. Accessed 25 January 2020.

6 Amazon. 2019. Renewable energy. *Sustainability—US*. Available at <https://sustainability.aboutamazon.com/

sustainable-operations/renewable-energy>. Accessed 28 December 2019.

7 Amazon Staff. "Amazon Wind and Solar Farms." *US About Amazon*, 8 Apr. 2019, www.aboutamazon.com/sustainability/energy-and-environment/amazon-wind-and-solar-farms.

8 Kara Hurst. 2019. 50 solar rooftops completed. *US Day One Blog.* Available at *<https://blog.aboutamazon.com/sustainability/50-solar-rooftops-completed>.* Accessed 28 December 2019.

9 Emily Esposito Fulkerson. 2019. Better packaging, happy pets, and a win for the environment. Available at *<https://blog.aboutamazon.com/sustainability/better-packaging-happy-pets-and-a-win-for-the-environment>.* Accessed 28 December 2019.

10 Neal Karlinsky. 2019. Reinventing an American icon. *US Day One Blog.* Available at *<https://blog.aboutamazon.com/sustainability/reinventing-an-american-icon>.* Accessed 28 December 2019.

11 Tom Murray. 2018. Amazon's Big Opportunity: Transparency In Sustainability. *Forbes.* Available at *<https://www.forbes.com/sites/edfenergyexchange/2018/04/02/amazons-big-opportunity-transparency-in-sustainability/#5cf239967c50>.* Accessed 2 January 2020.

12 Ibid.

13 Chen, Connie. 2019. Amazon Day is a new Prime-member perk from Amazon that allows you to schedule your package deliveries—here's how it works. *Business Insider.* Available at *<https://www.businessinsider.com/what-is-amazon-day-schedule-deliveries-prime-benefit>.* Accessed 2 January 2020.

14 Unilever. 2014. Operational highlights—At a glance | Sustainable living | Unilever Global. Available at *<https://*

web.archive.org/web/20140402110549/http://unilever.com/sustainable-living/ourapproach/ourbusinessataglance/>. Accessed 2 January 2020.

15 Schumpeter. 2017. The parable of St Paul. *The Economist*. Available at <*https://www.economist.com/business/2017/08/31/the-parable-of-st-paul*>. Accessed 2 January 2020.

16 "Our Strategy for Sustainable Growth." *Unilever Global Company Website, www.unilever.com/sustainable-living/our-strategy/*.

17 We Mean Business Coalition. 2019. Company Profile: Unilever. *We Mean Business Coalition*. Available at <*https://www.wemeanbusinesscoalition.org/blog/company-profile-unilever/*>. Accessed 2 January 2020.

18 Unilever. 2019. Waste & packaging. *Unilever global company website*. Available at <*https://www.unilever.com/sustainable-living/reducing-environmental-impact/waste-and-packaging/*>. Accessed 28 December 2019.

19 Unilever. 2019. Rethinking plastic packaging—towards a circular economy. *Unilever global company website*. Available at <*https://www.unilever.com/sustainable-living/reducing-environmental-impact/waste-and-packaging/rethinking-plastic-packaging/*>. Accessed 28 December 2019.

20 We Mean Business Coalition. 2019. Company Profile: Unilever. *We Mean Business Coalition*. Available at <*https://www.wemeanbusinesscoalition.org/blog/company-profile-unilever/*>. Accessed 2 January 2020.

21 Unilever. 2017. Unilever's Sustainable Living brands continue to drive higher rates of growth. *Unilever global company website*. Available at <*https://www.unilever.com/news/press-releases/2017/unilevers-sustainable-living-brands-continue-to-drive-higher-rates-of-growth.html*>. Accessed 28 December 2019.

22 Daphné Dupont-Nivet. 2017. Inside Unilever's sustainability myth. *New Internationalist*. Available at <https://newint.org/features/web-exclusive/2017/04/13/inside-unilever-sustainability-myth>. Accessed 2 January 2020.

23 "Our Strategy for Sustainable Growth." *Unilever Global Company Website, www.unilever.com/sustainable-living/our-strategy/*.

CHAPTER 16

1 US EPA, OAR. 2016. Global Greenhouse Gas Emissions Data. Overviews and Factsheets. *US EPA*. Available at <https://www.epa.gov/ghgemissions/global-greenhouse-gas-emissions-data>. Accessed 21 November 2019.

2 IPCC. 2014. *AR5 Climate Change 2014: Mitigation of Climate Change—IPCC*. Available at <https://www.ipcc.ch/report/ar5/wg3/>. Accessed 21 November 2019.

3 US EPA, OAR. 2017. *Sources of Greenhouse Gas Emissions*. Overviews and Factsheets. Available at <https://www.epa.gov/ghgemissions/sources-greenhouse-gas-emissions>. Accessed 21 November 2019.

4 Goldman Environmental Foundation. 2011. Ursula Sladek—Goldman Environmental Foundation: Goldman Environmental Foundation. Available at <https://www.goldmanprize.org/recipient/ursula-sladek/>. Accessed 3 January 2020.

5 EWS. n.d. International. *EWS Schönau*. Available at <https://www.ews-schoenau.de/ews/international/>. Accessed 3 January 2020.

6 Goldman Environmental Foundation. 2011. Ursula Sladek—Goldman Environmental Foundation: Goldman Environmental Foundation. Available at <https://www.

goldmanprize.org/recipient/ursula-sladek/>. Accessed 3 January 2020.

7 Ibid.

8 United Nations. 2010. *100% Renewable Electricity Supply by 2050 .:. Sustainable Development Knowledge Platform*. Sustainable Development Goals. Available at <*https://sustainabledevelopment.un.org/index.php?page=view&type=99&nr=24&menu=1449*>. Accessed 3 January 2020.

9 Robert Kunzing. 2015. Germany Has Some Revolutionary Ideas, and They're Working. *Magazine*. Available at <*https://www.nationalgeographic.com/magazine/2015/11/germany-renewable-energy-revolution/*>. Accessed 3 January 2020.

10 Christianson, Russ. n.d. Danish Wind Co-ops Can Show Us the Way: 6.

11 Ibid.

12 Jaime Lopez. 2013. Reforestation in Costa Rica: An Ongoing Effort. *Costa Rica Star News*. Available at <*https://news.co.cr/reforestation-in-costa-rica-an-ongoing-effort/23571/*>. Accessed 3 January 2020.

13 Sebastian Rodriguez. 2019. Costa Rica launches 'unprecedented' push for zero emissions by 2050—Reuters. Available at <*https://www.reuters.com/article/us-costa-rica-climatechange-transportati/costa-rica-launches-unprecedented-push-for-zero-emissions-by-2050-idUSKCN1QE253*>. Accessed 3 January 2020.

14 Marta Perez, and Orsibal Ramirez. 2018. EbA Evidence and Policy: Costa Rica. *International Institute for Environment and Development*. Available at <*https://www.iied.org/eba-evidence-policy-costa-rica*>. Accessed 25 January 2020.

15 Robert Blasiak. 2011. Ethics and environmentalism: Costa Rica's lesson—United Nations University. Available at <https://unu.edu/publications/articles/ethics-and-environmentalism-costa-ricas-lesson.html>. Accessed 12 January 2020.

16 Costa Rica. 2019. Costa Rica's Constitution of 1949 with Amendments through 2011. Available at <https://www.constituteproject.org/constitution/Costa_Rica_2011.pdf>. Accessed 12 January 2020.

17 Marta Perez, and Orsibal Ramirez. 2018. EbA Evidence and Policy: Costa Rica. *International Institute for Environment and Development.* Available at <https://www.iied.org/eba-evidence-policy-costa-rica>. Accessed 25 January 2020.

18 Samantha Cooper. 2019. Costa Rica's Zero-Carbon Plan Could Be a Model for the World. *Wired.* Available at <https://www.wired.com/story/costa-rica-zero-carbon-emissions-by-2050/>. Accessed 3 January 2020.

19 Ibid.

20 Nathaniel Keohane, and Dan J. Dudek. 2019. How cap and trade works. *Environmental Defense Fund.* Available at <https://www.edf.org/climate/how-cap-and-trade-works>. Accessed 12 January 2020.

21 C2ES. 2017. Market-Based State Policy. *Center for Climate and Energy Solutions.* Available at <https://www.c2es.org/content/market-based-state-policy/>. Accessed 29 October 2019.

22 Nathaniel Keohane, and Dan J. Dudek. 2019. How cap and trade works. *Environmental Defense Fund.* Available at <https://www.edf.org/climate/how-cap-and-trade-works>. Accessed 12 January 2020.

23 Seth Kerschner. 2017. United States: Greenhouse gas emissions trading schemes | Lexology. Available at <https://

www.lexology.com/library/detail.aspx?g=0f6bf054-27dd-4cc0-b856-107b1ad0854e>. Accessed 29 October 2019.

CONCLUSION

1 2020. How many planets does it take to sustain your lifestyle? Available at <http://www.footprintcalculator.org/>. Accessed 26 January 2020.

IMAGES PAGE 163

Nguyen, Caroline. 2017. Wangari Maathai: Environmental Leader, Feminist and Role Model. GreenPAC. [Photograph]. Available at <https://www.greenpac.ca/wangari_maathai_environmental_leader_feminist_and_role_model>. Accessed 27 March 2020.

May Boeve - Climate Change is Changing the World - We Too Must Change—Oct 2018. [Photograph]. Available at <https://www.youtube.com/watch?v=Etzxbp9E08k>. Accessed 27 March 2020.

2020. Greta Thunberg—Wikiquote. [Photograph]. Available at <https://en.wikiquote.org/wiki/Greta_Thunberg>. Accessed 27 March 2020.

Environmental Defense Fund. Home. Environmental Defense Fund. Available at <https://www.edf.org/home>. Accessed 27 March 2020.

N.d. See Jane Do: Ursula Sladek. [Photograph]. Available at <https://seejanedo.typepad.com/see_jane_do/ursula-sladek/>. Accessed 27 March 2020.

Mellon, Jayson. n.d. SLO lays out long-term path to get 70 percent of the way to its net-zero goal. New Times San Luis Obispo. [Photograph]. Available at <https://www.newtimesslo.com/sanluisobispo/slo-lays-out-long-term-

path-to-get-70-percent-of-the-way-to-its-net-zero-goal/ Content?oid=9116495>. Accessed 27 March 2020.

Mosely, Jamel. n.d. Leah Penniman on Why Farming Is an Act of Defiance for People of Color | Bon Appétit. [Photograph]. Available at *<https://www.bonappetit.com/story/leah-penniman-farming>*. Accessed 27 March 2020.

N.d. Extinction Rebellion | LinkedIn. Available at *<https://www.linkedin.com/company/extinction-rebellion>*. Accessed 27 March 2020.

www.ingramcontent.com/pod-product-compliance
Lightning Source LLC
LaVergne TN
LVHW012102070526
838200LV00074BA/3922